TRUE CRIME CASE HISTORIES

Volume 8

JASON NEAL

iDigital Group

Cover photos of:

Mikhail Drachev (top-left)

Gary Vinter (top-right)

Marty Dill (bottom-left)

Jared Chance (bottom-right)

Also by Jason Neal

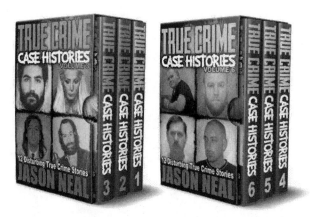

Looking for more?? I am constantly adding new volumes of True Crime Case Histories and all books are also available in paperback, hardcover and audiobooks.

Check out the complete series on Amazon:

Amazon US / Amazon UK

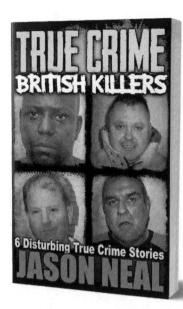

**FREE Bonus Book
For My Readers**

**Click to get
your free copy!**

As my way of saying "Thank you" for downloading, I'm giving away a FREE true crime book I think you'll enjoy.

http://truecrimecasehistories.com

Just click the link above to let me know where to send your free gift!

Choose Your Free True Crime Audiobook

Add Audible Narration and Keep the Story Going!
Plus Get a FREE True Crime Audiobook!

Switch between listening to an audiobook and reading on your
Kindle. **Plus choose your first audiobook for FREE!** Audible US /
Audible UK

CONTENTS

INTRODUCTION

When people learn that I'm a writer, most take an immediate interest. People are genuinely fascinated by others that have taken the time to write a book. However, the books I write are not novels and they're not for everyone. When a friend asks which of my books they should read first, I usually tell them that maybe they shouldn't read any of them. True crime is not for everyone. If someone is accustomed to reading steamy romances or cozy mysteries, true crime in general may not be the genre for that person.

True crime books are an entirely different animal, so I make certain the reader knows what they're getting into. Real true crime is not CSI. It's exponentially more horrible. True crime fans who have been reading these books for years already know this. Even television documentaries will skip over the truly gruesome parts of crime stories. In my books, I don't skip over the details no matter how disturbing they may be. My intent is to give the reader a better glimpse into the mind of the killer.

There are twelve stories in this volume of True Crime Case Histories. Arguably, the hardest part about writing true crime is finding stories that people haven't already heard. With the influx of true crime television shows and podcasts nowadays, that is a nearly impossible task. Luckily, my biggest asset is my readers. I count on *you* to provide me with story ideas that might not have been covered by major media outlets. If you ever have a lesser-known story that you think should be written about, please, please email it to me and I will do my best to research it.

One particular story in this volume was sent to me by several readers in the Michigan area. The news of a young woman's savage death in 2018 was front-page news in Michigan, but the rest of the world may not have heard the story yet.

In this volume, you'll read some stories that take place as recently as a few years ago while others date back as far as the 1930s. There's the story of a young Russian immigrant who came to the United States seeking the exciting lifestyle he'd seen on television, only to be stabbed, set on fire, and left to die in the desert by his own friends.

There's also the story of a brawny railway worker who couldn't control his steroid-fueled rage. After killing two people and being sentenced to life in prison, he continued his rage behind bars.

There's the story of a young woman who was abducted while sunbathing along the Ohio River. A witness across the river saw the abduction in progress and identified the abductor, but after more than twenty-five years, the girl's mother still searches for answers.

Some stories made major news headlines, like that of the awkward farm boy from British Columbia who preyed upon desperate prostitutes, killing as many as forty-nine women while leaving almost no trace of their remains.

The stories in this volume are shocking and exhibit human behavior at its absolute worst. Pure evil. However, these things really happen in the world. We may never understand what goes on in a killer's mind, but at least we can be better informed.

Lastly, I'd like to encourage you to sign up for my email newsletter for discounts, updates, and a free book. You can sign up here:

http://TrueCrimeCaseHistories.com

Thanks,

Jason

A CRUEL HOAX

Despite the freezing December chill, twenty-four-year-old Rebecca Koster wore only a black tank top under her black puffy jacket on the evening of December 3, 2009. She wanted to look sexy that night and she didn't have to work hard at it. Her petite frame, dark skin, and long, black, curly hair gave her an exotic look that attracted plenty of young men. She slipped her fur-topped boots over her tight light-blue jeans and sent a text message to her mother before she headed out to meet with her friends.

Rebecca's mother, Barbara Ross, was working the graveyard shift as a nurse at a nearby hospital that night. She made her daughter promise she would message her when she got back home safe and sound, just as she always had.

It was a Wednesday night in Medford, New York, on Long Island. Like her mother, Rebecca was in the healthcare industry. Rebecca worked as a home health aide for the elderly and autistic children and, even though she had to be at work the next morning at 6:00 A.M., she was out to have a good time that night. Sleep be damned.

Rebecca and her boyfriend, Dan Mayor, drove to Holbrook where they met with her friend, Nicole Longo, and another female friend for drinks. As the night progressed, the four of them moved on to a livelier bar called Butcher Boys Bar and Grill.

Rebecca Koster

She had only been dating twenty-eight-year-old Dan Mayor for two months. Dan was mesmerized by her dark brown eyes and infectious smile. He was in love. Rebecca, on the other hand, felt that the relationship was much more casual. To her, Dan was just a nice guy to hang out with and they got along fine. But as a long-term relationship—she wasn't too sure yet. She was young, beautiful, had a promising career, and men fawned over her. She had no intention of settling down anytime soon.

Rebecca and her friends drank, chatted, and mingled with the local crowd while Dan played pool and spoke with other friends in the bar. On several occasions, Rebecca had to chase away men who offered to buy her drinks. Her beauty stood out in a crowd, so she was used to the constant attention. However, she was a bit shocked when one man, a little more aggressive than the rest, took her cell phone from her hand after she shot him down, entered his phone number into it, and handed it back to her. Rebecca just rolled her eyes as he walked away.

By midnight, Nicole was ready to go home for the night. She had to work in the morning and so did Rebecca. But Rebecca was having too much fun. If she went home now, she would still only get a few hours of sleep. Why even bother? Nicole had planned on giving Rebecca a ride home that night, but they agreed that Dan could give her a ride home later.

It was 3:30 A.M. before Dan Mayor and two friends dropped Rebecca off at her home on Falcon Avenue. Immediately after getting home, she messaged her mother to let her know she was home safe, just as she had promised.

———

The next morning, when Barbara Ross got home from her shift at the hospital, she checked Rebecca's bedroom and saw that she was gone. "Good, she made it to work on time," she thought. But when her work called to find out where she was, Barbara's first instinct was anger. She assumed that Rebecca had stayed the night with Dan and slept in—that she had blown off work.

Barbara called Dan's cell phone when there was no answer from Rebecca, but she was confused—Dan claimed she wasn't with him. Barbara checked the garage and found Rebecca's car. In her bedroom, her purse lay on the dresser with her driver's license inside. Besides Rebecca herself, the only thing missing was her cell phone.

Barbara frantically called and texted her daughter's cell phone, but there was still no answer. She called Nicole and the other friends she had been out with that night, but nobody knew where she was. Barbara knew that Rebecca had made it home that night because she had texted and her purse was there, but sometime after 3:30 she had simply vanished.

Barbara and her husband, Larry Ross, immediately contacted the police to report their daughter missing, but Rebecca was twenty-four. Although she lived with her parents, she was an adult and was allowed to come and go as she pleased. The police said they would work on the case but suggested the family give her some more time. She was probably fine and would come home on her own.

Rebecca's family and friends were in no mood to wait. She was a responsible girl and there was no way she was fine if she hadn't contacted them. Something was undeniably wrong and they were all panic-stricken. Their home became a makeshift command center. Rebecca's friends and family gathered at the house, printed flyers, and went door to door in the area, hoping for any clue at all.

Rebecca and her family each had a smartphone app installed that tracked their location. Each time the app showed that her phone hit a cell phone tower, they could tell the approximate area of the phone. In 2009, the technology didn't give pinpoint accuracy, but it gave them at least some idea of where her phone was.

Each time there was a new ping from a cell tower, several members of her friends and family alerted the police and went to search the area. They knocked on doors and talked to anyone they could, but there was just no sign of her.

Her family and friends couldn't help but wonder if Dan Mayor had something to do with Rebecca's disappearance. After all, he was the last one to see her and none of them really knew him very well. They had only been dating for two months. He could have easily come back to the house after she had messaged her mother. Perhaps he was jealous of all the attention that Rebecca was getting at the bar that night. Some of the family members were becoming convinced that he was keeping her somewhere against her will.

———

After three days, Rebecca's family was losing hope when suddenly Barbara's cell phone chimed. At last, it was a text message from Rebecca. However, any sign of hopefulness quickly turned to terror when she read the message.

"Dan has me tied up in the basement. I think I'm in Commack."

Barbara immediately tried to call her but there was no answer. Then she messaged her back, "If you're able to message me… just call 911!"

Panicked, they notified the police and the entire group of family and friends rushed to Dan's house. When they arrived, the police were already there with grim looks on their faces. There was no sign of Rebecca. What's more, after questioning Dan, detectives didn't believe he was involved. He freely opened his house for them to search and was just as upset as Rebecca's family and friends. But some of the family members were still convinced that Dan was somehow involved.

When the text had come in, Rebecca's cell phone had pinged from Commack, twenty miles from their home. But when family members rushed over there, they found an industrial area strewn with warehouses and no sign of Rebecca. Then, just three hours after the first message, Barbara received another message:

"Don't tell Dan about my text message or he will kill me."

Again, Barbara messaged back telling her to call 911, but she was beginning to realize that the messages weren't coming from Rebecca at all. The messages didn't sound like her. They didn't seem as though they were written by someone who was in a panic. And if she could take the time to send a text message, why wouldn't she have just called 911? Barbara was beginning to realize it was all a cruel hoax.

Six days had passed since anyone had seen Rebecca. For a moment there was a glimmer of hope, but it was now clear that the text messages hadn't come from Rebecca at all. Someone had her phone and was toying with the family, putting them through unnecessary agony.

The agony was amplified with dread when police arrived at the family home asking for DNA and hair samples from Rebecca's hairbrush and toothbrush. The truth was, Rebecca had died before they even knew she was missing.

———

One day after Rebecca had gone missing, a brush fire was reported on the side of a road in North Sonnington, Connecticut, more than ninety miles from where Rebecca was last seen. When the fire department arrived, they realized that it wasn't a brush fire at all. It was a burning body.

For the next five days, the body had been listed as a Jane Doe. Her body had been wrapped in a blanket. A plastic bag was over her head and sealed at the neck with duct tape. She had been dumped on the side of the road, doused in a flammable liquid, and set on fire.

When medical examiners assessed what was left of the body, they found that all fingers and toes had been cut off and her face had been mutilated. Someone had cut off her ears and nose in an attempt to hide piercings. Large areas of skin on her back and one ankle were also cut away to remove tattoos. The missing pieces were not found at the scene. She had been stabbed in the liver and her throat had been cut, which were the wounds that eventually killed her.

It took five days to identify the body of Rebecca Koster. Five days of hell that the family had been put through. The hoax text messages that Rebecca's mother had received were sent two days after her death.

———

Rebecca Koster's family and friends were beyond shocked by the news of her death. They had held out hope that she would miraculously return but it wasn't to be. Not only had she died a horrible death, but the killer was still out there and had been playing a cruel, unnecessary joke on all of them. Most of them believed that horrible person to be Dan Mayor.

Investigators, however, were still collecting evidence and had their doubts that Dan had anything to do with the murder. If Dan was the killer, why would he have implicated himself in the text messages? It just didn't make sense.

Investigators sifted through hours of video footage from Butcher Boys Bar and Grill surveillance footage. On the night Rebecca went missing, many men were seen approaching her and speaking briefly to her, but the one who grabbed her phone stood out. He was aggressive and Rebecca seemed annoyed at the altercation. The video footage, however, wasn't enough to identify who he actually was. All they could tell was that he was a large African-American male.

Detectives pulled Rebecca's cell phone records and found that just after she arrived home at 3:30 that morning, she received a phone call from a phone number with a Boston prefix. She didn't answer the first time it rang, but when the person called back at 4:15 A.M., she answered and spoke to the person for twenty minutes. The clue, however, was a dead end. The phone was a pre-paid burner phone and there was no record of who had purchased it. Police believed the call was from the mysterious man that had grabbed Rebecca's phone at the bar on the night she went missing. He had likely texted himself from her phone so he could get her phone number. Rebecca's friends, however, had no idea who the man was. They had never seen him before.

One piece of evidence from the crime scene, however, proved to be useful. The duct tape that held the plastic bag around her head. Investigators were able to pull a fingerprint from the duct tape: it belonged to thirty-year-old Evans Ganthier from Central Islip, just seven miles from the Butcher Boys Bar and Grill.

Evans Ganthier

Evans Ganthier was an unemployed graduate of Dowling College, where he received a bachelor's degree in psychology. Although he had no prior police record, a New York State business registration under the name Secrets Adult Entertainment Services suggested he may have been involved in some sort of escort agency. Perhaps he was trying to recruit Rebecca.

Ganthier matched the video footage from the bar surveillance video. Another security video from the early morning ferry from Long Island to Connecticut showed Evans Ganthier in his mother's SUV on the morning of December 4. It turned out Rebecca's dismembered body had been in the back of the SUV as he took that ferry to Connecticut. When the body had been found later that day, Ganthier had been checked into a hotel just around the corner.

When Ganthier was arrested on February 8, 2010, he freely admitted that he put his phone number into Rebecca Koster's cell phone that night and called her at 4:15 A.M. It's unknown how he lured her out of her house, but Ganthier claimed that Rebecca got into his car willingly. As they drove, he claimed that Rebecca began gagging and foaming at the mouth. Not knowing what to do, he told detectives that he took her to his house rather than taking her to a hospital.

Ganthier explained that he opened the garage door of his house and had planned to enter the house through the garage, but Rebecca tripped over barbells on his garage floor and hit her head on the floor. Ganthier claimed that she was bleeding profusely from the head and he put her back into his car to take her to the hospital, but she died on the way. The autopsy, however, showed he was lying. Rebecca had died from knife wounds to her neck and liver. There had been no sign of blunt force trauma to her head.

When detectives asked why he cut off her fingers, toes, ears, and nose and ripped the tattoos from her back and ankle, he replied, "I had the knife in my hand. I made a mistake. I can't take it back." Ganthier claimed her death was an accident and he only cut her up to hide her identity. He admitted that he then put her in the back of his mother's SUV and took a ferry to Connecticut, dumped her body, and set it on fire. Ganthier had no excuse for why he had taunted the family by texting them after her death. Detectives believed it was a feeble an attempt to throw off the investigation with no consideration of the family's emotions.

Four and a half years after her death, Rebecca Koster's killer, Evans Ganthier, was tried and convicted of second-degree murder. He received the maximum penalty of twenty-five years to life in prison. Rebecca's family will be waiting to protest when Ganthier is up for parole in 2023.

2

THE MUSCLEBOUND MURDERER

Twenty-two-year-old Carl Edon worked the graveyard shift repairing commuter trains for a rail company in northern England. During his shifts, he worked alone in a small workshop alongside the quiet rail tracks near the Grangetown train depot. At home, Carl's girlfriend, Michelle Robertson, took care of their two-year-old son. Michelle was pregnant and the couple were expecting a beautiful baby girl in just a few short months. As Carl worked alone in his workshop in the late hours of August 2, 1995, a co-worker, Douglas "Gary" Vinter, stopped by for a visit.

Gary Vinter worked for the same rail company. Also on the graveyard shift, Vinter worked as signal box operator a short distance down the tracks from Carl. His job was to change the direction of the tracks for each train that went by at the junction to ensure each train made it to its proper destination. The late hours were quiet that Wednesday night, however. With no trains due for a while, Vinter had time to walk down the tracks to chat with Carl in his small workshop.

At six-foot-seven, Gary Vinter was a massive man with shoulders so wide one might think he would need to turn sideways to get through a doorway. He was well-known as a barroom brawler with a short temper and his immense size gave him an advantage. It's not known what the topic of conversation was that warm August night between Carl and Vinter, but something that was said set Vinter off. Something lit a fuse inside his brain that could only be put out one way —with death.

Vinter later told police that Carl had provoked him and came at him with a knife, but he was no match for Vinter's muscle. Vinter overpowered his co-worker, took the knife from him, and stabbed him repeatedly. When the knife hit bone and broke, Vinter looked through drawers in the workshop, found another knife, and continued his bloody rampage. By the time he was finished, Carl Edon had been stabbed thirty-seven times. Every one of his internal organs had been punctured.

With the knife still sticking in Edon's lifeless body, Vinter left the workshop, walked back to his signal box, and made sure the tracks were positioned correctly for the next several trains. He then drove to a nearby police station to report that he'd killed a man.

Gary Vinter drew the arresting officer a map so they could find the tiny workshop and told police that they should inform his employer that the signal box was unattended. He was concerned that trains may crash in his absence if the tracks weren't changed for each train.

Although he admitted that he had killed Edon, he refused to admit that it was murder. Vinter claimed that Edon had ridiculed him and provoked him. The only crime he was willing to admit to was manslaughter.

Two months after Carl Edon's death, his partner Michelle gave birth to their daughter. She named her Carla, in memory of Carl.

———

Despite his claim of manslaughter, Vinter was charged with murder. The prosecution told the court that an assault where someone breaks a knife while stabbing someone, then seeks out another knife to continue the killing, does not fall under the definition of manslaughter—it was cold blooded murder.

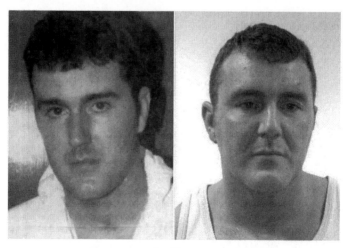

Gary Vinter

The court agreed and in May 1996, Gary Vinter was found guilty and sentenced to life in prison. But in many countries, unfortunately, life does not necessarily mean life. Vinter's sentence was eventually reduced to twelve years. In the end, he served less than ten years.

————

During his years in prison, Gary Vinter was a model prisoner. He didn't cause trouble and spent most of his time working out in the prison gym. What prison employees didn't know was that Vinter had access to anabolic steroids, even behind bars. He became obsessed with building his already massive body into a muscle-bound killing machine.

From 2003 until his release in 2006, Vinter was allowed periodic "home visits." It was a program for prisoners that were in their final years of incarceration and had exhibited good behavior. Vinter was allowed outside of the prison walls for short periods of time—usually seventy-two hours. During his years in prison, he began communicating with Anne White, a mother of four in her late thirties. Over time, their letters and her visits to the prison grew into a romantic relationship. During Vinter's home visits, he spent most of his time with Anne and they eventually married in July 2006, just after his release from prison.

Anne's friends and family were less than happy about her new relationship with the convicted killer. Anne was a grown woman, however, and there wasn't much they were able to say or do to stop her.

Vinter had been out of prison for less than six months before he was in trouble again. On the evening of New Year's Eve 2006, he was out celebrating at The Miners Arms pub near his home when a fight broke out between Vinter and three other men. In the fray, Vinter was hit in the back of the head with a pint glass and he flew into a steroid- and alcohol-fueled rage. As the fight made its way onto the sidewalk, security cameras captured Vinter beating forty-year-old Geoffrey Ewart to the ground. There were no major injuries to anyone involved but the attack was enough to send Vinter back to prison.

Again, Vinter was on his best behavior. He was a model prisoner and spent his time working out in the gym. In December 2007, Vinter was released from prison for the second time, just in time for Christmas.

By late January, Anne White had been living with him for only a month but knew she had made a mistake by marrying Gary Vinter. She confided to her close friends that she was unhappy in her marriage but was afraid to leave Vinter because of his obvious anger issues. Every text message she received, no matter who it was from, threw him into a jealous rage. Vinter couldn't stand that Anne had a life outside of him. As a result, she had become the target of his growing anger.

On February 6, his frustration with their marital issues had reached a boiling point. At the end of an evening of screaming at each other, Vinter smashed the television and stormed out of the house. On his way out the door, he took Anne's passport—just to make sure she didn't venture too far.

For each of the next five nights away from home, Vinter's jealousy grew. He went from pub to pub, desperately looking for his wife. He knew that he would eventually find her out drinking with friends. Or worse, with another man.

On February 11, thirty-eight-year-old Vinter, with his two younger friends, found Anne at The Miners Arms—the same pub where he had the brawl that sent him back to prison. When Vinter entered the pub and confronted Anne, it only took minutes for the couple to begin screaming at each other inside the pub.

Vinter's young friends, both just twenty-two years old, tried to calm him down but his anger had gotten out of control. He grabbed Anne by the upper arm and dragged her outside to his friend's car. He pushed her into the back seat and screamed at his two friends to drive to his mother's house, just a mile away. As Anne and Vinter exited the vehicle at his mother's house, she said to the young men, "you don't know what you're getting yourself into being with him."

Back at the pub, Anne's friends were worried sick. Her hulk-like husband had dragged her out of the pub in a fury. When they called her cell phone, they were surprised that she answered in a calm voice. Anne told her friends that she and Gary were just at another pub drinking and having fun. Despite her calm demeanor, her friends could tell she was lying. They suspected she was just trying to settle down her hostile husband. Scared for her safety, they called police.

Sadly, her friends were right. Unfortunately, her words didn't rectify his anger. Moments after the call, Vinter strangled his wife in his mother's kitchen while his mother slept upstairs. But his massive hands squeezing around her throat couldn't kill her, so Vinter found a kitchen knife. He stabbed her once in the heart and four times in the lung. Like the prior murder, Vinter used two knives in the attack, the first of which broke when it hit bone. Once she was dead, he left her bleeding out on the kitchen floor.

Vinter called his two young friends and told them to come back to his mother's house to pick him up. With his hands and shirt still covered in blood, he got into the car and yelled, "GO, GO, GO!" and they sped off into the night.

Later that night, as they drove through the dark city, Vinter used Anne's phone to call police:

"Right, my name is Gary Vinter. I'm solely responsible for the death of my wife. There's nobody else involved. Just me. I killed my wife. That's all I'm prepared to say."

When police finally caught up with Vinter at 2:00 A.M., despite his admission of the murder, it took several officers with batons to control the massive man. Once he was subdued, Vinter said:

"I'm a convicted murderer. Nobody's going to take a blind bit of notice of what I've got to say. I'll be pleading guilty at the earliest opportunity. I will not be running a trial."

During his interrogation, Vinter gave no reason for the crime other than stating:

"The reasons I did it? Well, I'll be keeping that to myself."

Vinter pleaded guilty to the murder. At his sentencing, Judge Peter Fox told Vinter:

"Regrettably, you are incapable of self-control. Your extreme violence to others cannot be viewed as other than contin- uing for as far as can be seen. You therefore fall into that relatively small category of people who should be deprived permanently of their liberty in a civilized society. It is a whole life sentence."

Although Vinter had been handed his second life sentence, that would not be the end of his mayhem.

In March 1995, an eight-year-old girl was abducted and sexually assaulted in Crawley, UK. Three months later, a man named Roy Whiting confessed to the crime. Although he faced a potential life sentence for the crime, Whiting was given only four years in prison because he had confessed. Although he was deemed likely to commit more crimes by psychologists, he was released after serving only two years and five months of his sentence.

Less than three years later, Roy Whiting abducted, sexually assaulted, and murdered another eight-year-old, Sarah Payne, while she played near her grandparents' home. For that crime, Whiting was serving a life sentence at the Wakefield Prison in West Yorkshire: the same prison that held Gary Vinter.

In July 2011, using a toilet brush that had been broken and sharpened into a shank, Gary Vinter attacked and stabbed Roy Whiting several times. When he fell to the ground, Vinter punched and kicked him repeatedly, yelling, "You stupid fucking nonce!"

A small piece of the plastic shank broke inside Whiting's eye socket. Vinter said of the attack, "The only reason he's still alive is because I got tired." Vinter was given another five-year jail term for the attack—not that it made a difference.

In the late 1980s, Lee Newell strangled his fifty-six-year-old neighbor and stuffed her body into a cupboard while he robbed her home. He managed to get away with a whopping £60. While serving a life sentence for the crime, he and another inmate murdered a different inmate named Subhan Anwar. It's unclear if the murder was race related or if it was simply because Anwar was a child killer.

Throughout 2014, both Lee Newell and Gary Vinter were housed in the special segregation wing at Milton Keynes prison. Ever obsessed with his muscles, Vinter had requested repeatedly to be transferred to another prison with better gym facilities. However, he became frustrated when prison officials ignored his requests.

In November 2014, without provocation, Vinter punched Newell to the ground in the exercise yard as security cameras watched. Once on the ground, he repeatedly kicked Newell in the head, leaving him with a skull fracture, brain injuries, and permanently blind in one eye.

Vinter was charged with attempted murder for the vicious attack. The judge told him:

> "You were prepared to sacrifice the life of a fellow human being just so you could move prisons. What you did was pre-planned as part of your scheme. You must be one of the most dangerous individuals within the prison system today. Your record is truly shocking."

Vinter most likely only took the judge's comments in stride, as he had nothing to lose. He was given a third life sentence for the attack.

Amazingly, Vinter and two other murderers successfully appealed their whole life sentences, arguing that their life sentences were "inhuman and degrading." Although they were not released, the taxpayers of the United Kingdom were stuck with a bill of £34,471 to cover the cost of his appeal.

3

FOSSIL CREEK

On Christmas Day in 1991, the hammer and sickle flag was lowered for the final time over the Kremlin and the three striped Russian flag took its place. The Soviet empire had collapsed. Throughout the remainder of the decade, American television and movies took over the airwaves in the former Soviet Republic.

Most of what Konstantin Simberg knew about the United States was from what he saw on MTV from his home in Rostv-on-Don, an industrial town near what is now Ukraine. To the teenager, America was all about sexy girls, making easy money, and driving fast cars. It's no wonder that, when he and his parents moved to the United States in early 2000, he dressed in baggy pants, yellow-tinted glasses, and t-shirts advertising skateboard companies.

Simberg's parents had relatives living in the Phoenix area of the United States and took the opportunity to immigrate when it presented itself. They desperately wanted to provide a life for their son that was better than what they had in

Russia. But it wasn't to be. In the end, Konstantin's life couldn't have been more tragic.

———

Nineteen-year-old Simberg hadn't prepared well for the transition to American life. He spent most of his teenage years dreaming of America but had neglected to take the time to learn English. When he arrived in the United States, his broken English kept him from making many friends apart from other Soviet-bloc immigrants.

In June 2000, just six months after arriving in Phoenix, Simberg's Russian friends—that he had met while at a warehouse rave party—invited him to a birthday party of another Russian immigrant, Kseniya Vybornova.

It was Kseniya's twentieth birthday. She was a stunning blonde that worked as a stripper at Christie's Cabaret, an enormous high-end strip club in central Phoenix known for its opulent decor and beautiful dancers.

Simberg was immediately in love. It took some time for Kseniya to warm up to him, but eventually she and Simberg began dating and both of them fell head-over-heels. Kseniya had moved to the United States in the late 90s. Her older sister, Olga, had been living in the Phoenix area for several years when she convinced her sister to immigrate.

Olga told Kseniya, "The world is going to end because of Y2K. You must come to America. This is your last chance to see me." Olga was an equally gorgeous blonde who also danced at Christie's and had a brief career as a television news personality.

Kseniya and Olga had a strange living arrangement with Olga's boyfriend, Sean Southland. When Olga first met Southland, she saw that he rented a nice apartment and drove a BMW 750. To the young and naive girl, that defined him as a successful American businessman.

It was Southland that first suggested the two sisters work as strippers. His ex-wife had worked at the same club years earlier and made money hand-over-fist. Kseniya and Olga were knockouts and he knew they could make more than his ex-wife. By the time Kseniya had met Konstantin Simberg, the girls were making over $1,000 a night and living with Southland. Southland thought of himself as a manager for the two young girls. "Just hand all of the money you make over to me and I'll handle everything. We'll live like one big happy family and I'll be the man of the house."

Southland presented himself as a visionary businessman. But many that knew him said his real talent was talking people out of their money. He had served briefly in the US Army, where he claimed to have studied Russian at an elite "spy school" and served as a military intelligence specialist. He was discharged from the military for unknown reasons and hired as a Los Angeles police officer, where he was released after eighteen months. Again, for unknown reasons.

Southland had various failed business ventures but, when he met Troy Langdon in 1999, he was touting his business concept called "Sea Castle." Sea Castle was a business idea where the company would sell timeshares in multi-million-dollar yachts to those who craved the luxury but couldn't afford to buy an entire yacht themselves. Southland was seeking wealthy investors and Langdon was interested.

Troy Langdon ran a business in North Scottsdale, Arizona, called Peak Physique. The name made it sound like a gym but it was actually a pharmacy that catered to bodybuilders. His product was Human Growth Hormone (HGH).

At the time, HGH was an FDA-approved drug that pharmacies were allowed to market for only two uses: dwarfism in children and to control wasting in AIDS patients. Although pharmacies were limited in their distribution, doctors, however, could prescribe the drug however they liked. There were no restrictions.

On the open market, HGH was an extremely popular anti-aging drug. The pituitary gland naturally produces Human Growth Hormone. But when a study showed that injecting HGH improved muscle tone and body composition in twelve men, the market for the drug went wild. Despite potential side-effects of diabetes, swelling, high blood-pressure, and heart failure, every athlete and bodybuilder in the country wanted it.

Troy Langdon was a middle-man of sorts. His in-laws owned Cactus Pharmacy, which was a wholesale pharmacy that supplied retail pharmacies. They acquired the HGH but it was Langdon's company, Peak Physique, located next-door, that was able to sell it.

The late 90s was a boom for Langdon. In 1999, his business had almost no competition at all and, at its peak, was grossing $25 million a month. Langdon told Rolling Stone magazine, "HGH manufacturers had a monster sitting there and they couldn't do anything with it. But they could provide it in bulk to a guy like me, who'd go out there and sell it far and wide."

Langdon and Sean Southland had become close friends. In 1999, Langdon hired Southland to work for him for $10,000 per month, helped him purchase a home, and invested heavily in his yacht-share business idea. The two lived large with their new-found wealth and spent money on fast cars, expensive watches, cruising on yachts, and sipping champagne at strip clubs.

———

Kseniya had been living with her sister and Southland when she met Simberg, but Southland immediately disliked him. To Southland, Simberg was intruding on the money-making arrangement he had with the two naïve sisters. The last thing he wanted was for Kseniya to have a boyfriend. He didn't trust Simberg and told Kseniya he wasn't welcome in their home. Southland argued with Kseniya and urged her to dump him but it wasn't going to happen. Simberg was a hopeless romantic and good to her. She was in love.

Eventually, Kseniya moved out of the house and she and Simberg shared a small apartment. Money, however, was tight. Simberg wasn't working and, at his urging, Kseniya had quit her job as a stripper. The arrangement did, however, help the relationship between Simberg and Southland. The two couples socialized together and Simberg found a friend in Southland, who spoke fluent Russian.

———

For a brief time, Troy Langdon was on top of the world. His HGH business had been making him ludicrous amounts of money and everything he touched seemed to turn to gold. But just a year later, in the summer of 2000, competitors in his industry grew out of the woodwork. Suddenly Langdon was hemorrhaging money and selling his HGH with almost no markup. What had once been a life of luxury had become stress over debts owed to suppliers. Peak Physique was struggling just trying to stay afloat.

Southland, however, came up with an idea to save the company. Or at least buy them some time. The plan was simple—hire some kids to rob the FedEx truck that held one of their big shipments just before it was delivered. They could keep the "stolen" shipment, sell it on the black market, and have the whole cost of the shipment replaced by their insurance company.

In mid-September 2001, Troy Langdon called his suppliers of HGH and placed his largest order ever. 6,000 vials of Saizan HGH. On the black market, it could fetch over $3 million. Meanwhile, Southland recruited Simberg to put together a crew of young men to hijack the FedEx truck. Simberg would receive $20,000 for his part in the robbery and chose six friends he knew from the local rave scene, some of them still in high school.

Troy Langdon, Konstantin Simberg, & Sean Southland

On September 24, 2001, Konstantin Simberg and his friends watched as the FedEx truck delivering the HGH shipment drove towards Langdon's pharmacy. When the truck entered the parking lot, Simberg quickly pulled up in front of the truck in his old Chevy Camaro with its missing hood, blocking the truck from entering. Running from his Camaro, Simberg went up to the driver's side of the truck and, rather than point the BB gun he had purchased from Walmart at the driver, made him a simple proposition: he offered the driver $50,000 to let them take the shipment.

The FedEx driver was smart. He could see that these "robbers" were young and barely men at all. They clearly didn't intend to use deadly force. The driver stalled for time, argued with them, and eventually refused to allow them to take the shipment. Frustrated, Simberg and the other young men fled in frustration and the FedEx driver called the police.

Southland and Langdon were furious. Simberg had botched the job and they were still neck-deep in debt. The next day, Langdon increased the pharmacy's theft insurance coverage. Langdon, Southland, and Simberg would have to find another way. Southland gave Simberg a list of things to buy: glass cutters, gloves, and a crowbar. They planned to stage a robbery at the pharmacy. Two days after the failed robbery, Langdon sold the shipment he had just received to a local wholesaler but kept the transaction off the books.

———

Darrin Swenson was still in high school when Simberg had recruited him to be a part of the FedEx heist. Lured by the thought of making $700 for less than an hour of his time, he took part in the robbery. But afterwards, riddled with guilt, he went home and told his mother what he had done.

Darrin's mother convinced her son to call Phoenix police and report what he and the other young men had done.

Darrin explained that he had been hired by a friend, a Russian immigrant named Konstantin Simberg, but the "big boss" was a man that drove a black BMW 750 with dark tinted windows. He had seen the car pull up to talk to Simberg just before the attempted heist.

———

In the early hours of October 2nd, the burglar alarm went off at Cactus Pharmacy, Langdon's in-law's pharmacy next-door to Peak Physique. Simberg and Southland first tried to use the glass cutter but it wasn't as easy as it had seemed in the movies. Frustrated, they instead broke the window with the crowbar. Police arrived to find the broken window but the motion sensors showed no one had actually entered the pharmacy. When Troy Langdon arrived just minutes later, he informed police that they had to have gone inside somehow because eighteen boxes of his product had been stolen.

Detectives questioned Troy Langdon at the scene about the robbery but were immediately suspicious. The whole story reeked of an inside-job. Not trusting his story, detectives followed Langdon as he left the pharmacy. He drove his Porsche 911 to Village Inn, an all-night diner, where he met with Southland in his black BMW 750 with dark tinted windows. The same car that Darrin Swenson had claimed the "big boss" drove.

Detectives were still following Southland early that morning when he met up with Simberg in a parking lot in Phoenix.

———

It didn't take long for detectives to figure out what was going on and Langdon, Southland, and Simberg were arrested simultaneously the following day.

Langdon admitted nothing and claimed he had no knowledge of the botched heist or the idea that the burglary was an inside job. The detective, however, had already spoken to the Drug Enforcement Agency. They had been investigating Troy Langdon for quite some time.

Southland had a much more elaborate story. Although he seemed composed and cooperative, he refused to give any information. He claimed that he was bound to secrecy because he was working with the CIA.

Detective Tom Britt didn't believe a word from either of them. Konstantin Simberg, however, was much more cooperative. During his interrogation, Simberg fell apart. He cried as he spoke to Britt and told every detail of the crime.

Over time, Britt and Simberg became unlikely friends. Britt spoke fluent Russian and knew that Simberg was a pawn in the whole operation. Britt knew Langdon and Southland were running the show. All three were initially released without charges but knew they were coming.

———

With the news of Southland and Langdon's arrest, investors in Sea Castle were growing anxious. They wanted their money back. Among those investors was Simberg's girlfriend, Kseniya, who had invested $35,000 but knew it was unlikely she would ever see a return.

In early December, Simberg turned twenty-one. He and Kseniya were sick of the life they had created in Phoenix and the two of them dreamed of moving to New York City. But neither of them were working and both were out of cash. They needed to get Kseniya's $35,000 back from Southland.

On December 10, Simberg took a stand. He confronted both Langdon and Southland and demanded they return Kseniya's money. Simberg admitted that he had been talking to detectives about the robbery but, if they would just return the money, he and Kseniya would leave town and they would never see either of them again.

Simberg had been speaking to Detective Britt on a near daily basis for the past two months and the two had become good friends. But on December 14, Britt knew something was wrong. He received a phone call from Simberg but the call was from a phone number that he didn't recognize. Britt put him briefly on hold but when he clicked back to the call, he only heard him Simberg screaming and a scuffle in the background. Then the phone went dead.

———

100 miles north of Phoenix, Fossil Creek runs through the Coconino National Forest near Camp Verde, Arizona. Two days after Britt heard Simberg's screams, two hunters came across a badly burned body on the banks of the river. It was the body of Konstantin Simberg. He had been stabbed, soaked in gasoline, set on fire, and covered with large rocks.

Suspicion immediately fell on Southland and Langdon. Investigators already knew they had a reason to get rid of Simberg, but they had no proof.

It wasn't hard for investigators to get information about Simberg's last day alive. The phone call that Simberg made to Britt was traced back to the cell phone of eighteen-year-old

Chris Andrews. Andrews was a clean-cut, upper-middle-class student at Arizona State University. Andrews shared an apartment with an eighteen-year-old high school student named Mikhail Drachev. A search of the apartment revealed evidence of a bank transaction that had occurred just twenty minutes before Simberg had called Detective Britt.

Police searched through surveillance video at the bank, which showed Andrews and Drachev with Simberg and Dennis Tsoukanov, a twenty-year-old Estonian immigrant. Police believed some sort of transaction had gone wrong and the three men killed Simberg.

On January 14 Andrews, Drachev and Tsoukanov were charged with first-degree murder and kidnapping. However, by that time Andrews and Drachev had fled. The two had sold everything they owned, bought a beat-up Mercedes, and drove to New York. When they arrived, they went their own ways: Andrews flew to Spain and Drachev continued driving to Canada.

Potentially facing the death penalty, Dennis Tsoukanov immediately took a plea deal. He pleaded guilty to second degree murder in exchange for his testimony. What investigators really wanted to know was this: had the three boys been hired by Langdon and Southland to murder Simberg? They had no evidence for the accusation but it all seemed too convenient. Simberg had been brutally murdered just days after threatening to testify against them.

Tsoukanov explained that on December 14, Simberg and the three men went to the bank so Simberg could sign his Camaro over to Andrews. They had planned to take out a title loan on the vehicle and split the money, but Simberg had $400 in unpaid parking fines and the loan was denied. Andrews was furious.

The four men drove back to Andrews's apartment ,where Simberg had called Detective Britt. While he was on hold waiting for Britt to pick up, Andrews put on a pair of brass knuckles and beat him in the back of the head. The three men then gagged Simberg, bound his wrists and legs with duct tape, and threw him in a closet where he stayed for almost twenty-four hours.

The next day, they removed Simberg from the closet, blindfolded him, and walked him to the car. They told him,

> "We're going to drive you down to Mexico and let you go. Don't come back. Once you get there, you're on your own."

Simberg remained blindfolded as they drove through the desert for almost two hours. But when they arrived at the remote location of Fossil Creek in northern Arizona and removed Simberg's blindfold, he said, "Hey, this isn't Mexico."

They offered Simberg a "last cigarette," but he refused. He knew they were going to kill him. Andrews pulled out a TEC-9 semi-automatic pistol that he had purchased the day before, pressed it to Simberg's temple, and pulled the trigger. But the gun jammed.

They then tried to cut his throat with a hunting knife, but Simberg deflected the attack and the knife instead sliced him across the chin. There was no way Simberg could fend off three attackers and eventually he was stabbed in the back. The knife had punctured his lung.

But Simberg still didn't die. Andrews, Tsoukanov, and Drachev couldn't handle watching the blood spurt from the hole in his back, waiting for him to die. They poured gasoline over him as he squirmed on the ground and lit him on fire. They then covered him with large rocks in an attempt to hide the body but the rocks weren't enough. Simberg wasn't dead yet.

After the three killers had fled, Simberg pushed the rocks off of his body. The duct tape on his wrists had melted along with his flesh, meaning he was able to pull his still-burning jeans off of his legs. Simberg managed to crawl to the creek, thinking that the water would relieve his burns, but it was too late. He crawled to a tree near the banks of the creek and died.

———

Chris Andrews called his parents from Spain and swore to them that he had nothing to do with the murder. His parents talked him into coming back to Arizona and he was immediately arrested. Mikhail Drachev, however, was still on the run.

Mikhail Drachev, Chris Andrews & Dennis Tsoukanov

Langdon and Southland were never charged with the murder. There was no definitive proof that they were involved. For the robbery, Langdon pled down to a charge of Fraudulent Schemes and received no jail time. Five years later, Southland was found guilty of conspiracy and a drug violation and was sentenced to five years in prison. After his release, he was arrested again in New York, trying to smuggle six kilos of cocaine across the Canadian border. Trying to explain away the cocaine arrest, he told authorities he was working with the DEA and handed them Detective Britt's business card. It didn't work.

Dennis Tsoukanov was sentenced to thirteen years in prison for second degree murder and an additional ten years for kidnapping. He has since been released from prison. Chris Andrews was found guilty of first-degree murder and kidnapping and sentenced to life in prison.

Mikhail Drachev was still at large but was tried and found guilty without his presence. If authorities could just catch him, they could send him to prison. Despite being featured on the television show America's Most Wanted five times, there was just no sign of him.

Six years later, in 2007, Mikhail Drachev was living under an assumed name in Toronto, Canada. He had just proposed to his girlfriend of three years and she happily said "Yes." However, he had a surprise for her. He told her his real name.

Startled by his secrecy, she googled his name and found the America's Most Wanted website. The girl held her tongue for a week before walking into the police station to tell the police who her fiancée really was.

When police took Drachev away, he gave his fiancée a long kiss and told her he wasn't mad at her. He fought extradition for three years before he was finally returned to Arizona for sentencing.

Drachev pled guilty to second-degree murder, aggravated assault, and kidnapping. He will be eligible for release in 2042.

4

SLAYER'S BOOK OF DEATH

J ason Massey was one of seven children born to a
drug-addicted mother in 1973 in Huntsville, Texas.
Child protective services had taken away five of her
children before his birth, leaving Jason and his sister,
Johnia, to grow up without their siblings throughout the
1970s. Although he was never really sure who his biological
father was, his only memory of a father was that of being
beaten by him. Even as an infant, Jason's mother often left
the children alone in her parked car while she went to bars to
meet men in hopes they would buy her drinks and supply
her with drugs.

The idea of "home" was a fluid situation. The family
constantly moved from home to home, sometimes staying
with relatives or in motel rooms, often living in a car. When
they did have a home, Jason's mother would often leave for
hours on end and hide the only food in the house in her own
bedroom. If the children were caught entering her bedroom,
they would be beaten with a belt or a wooden paddle. On the
rare occasion that his mother hired a babysitter, Jason later

revealed that the male babysitter she hired had sexually abused him.

Jason's grandmother was an Evangelical Christian with a loose interpretation of the Bible. Though not abusive, she filled his head with stories of Satan, hell, and demons, to the point that Jason believed demons talked to him.

To put it mildly, early life was hell for Jason Massey. As a result, he had developed strong anti-social behaviors even before his teen years. He often arrived at school unwashed and underfed with visible bruises all over his body. His method of coping with living the life of a victim was to become the victimizer himself. Even at an early age, he bullied and beat up younger children, once pinning down a smaller boy and beating him with the branch of a tree. But Jason's favorite pastime was torturing and mutilating small animals. While other young boys in Texas learned to hunt for food with their fathers, Massey hunted to feed sadistic sexual urges that festered inside him. The thought of death excited him, while the pain of others seemed to empower him.

Jason Massey's definition of love was drastically flawed as well. At just twelve years old, he fell in love with a young girl from school named Anita Mendoza. But when she wanted nothing to do with him, he had no idea how to deal with that emotion. The rejection ate at him. He stalked the girl, repeatedly made obscene and threatening phone calls to her, and gave her notes telling her that he had dreams of killing her, slitting her throat, and drinking her blood. After she refused to date him, Massey butchered her dog and smeared its blood on the family's car.

In his early teenage years, Jason experimented with drugs and alcohol, which eventually became an everyday occurrence for him. His interests leaned towards heavy metal music, Satanism, and serial killers. He idolized notorious killers of the time, such as Charles Manson, Ted Bundy, and Henry Lee Lucas. These were men he admired and aspired to be like.

Jason Massey was sixteen years old when he dropped out of high school and found work as a roofer. That was also when he began keeping diaries in spiral bound notebooks. On the cover he titled them "The Slayer's Book of Death - Volumes 1-4. The Thoughts of Jason Massey." with the lettering in the font of one of his favorite heavy metal bands, Slayer.

Two years later, Jason's mother found the diaries and was shocked at the disturbing, violent content. The four notebooks contained over 500 pages of Massey's sadistic fantasies. In that moment, she knew something was terribly wrong with her young son.

Jason Massey & his Slayer's Book of Death

Jason Massey's notebooks went into great detail about his obsession with becoming a serial killer. "My goal is to kill 700 people in twenty years. I'm tired of feeling like shit for not being able to kill," he wrote. He also wrote of his need to "engrave his name on society," his desire to "lash out at society," and to "reap immense sorrow and suffering." He wrote of his fantasy of eating a girl's brain and heart and drinking her blood. The pages also told the story of how he killed Anita Mendoza's dog and smeared its blood on the family car.

The journals had singled-out girls that he knew from school and listed them as his future kill targets. All of them were between the ages of ten and thirteen. He had described how he loved each girl but needed to "possess" them; the only way he could do that was by killing them. To him, it was the only way that he could "be a man."

Massey listed the number of animals he had killed to date: forty-one cats, thirty-two dogs, and seven cows. He removed the heads of each one as a trophy.

He had written that he was learning as much as he could about police procedures so that he wouldn't get caught after the killings.

The most disturbing part of the journals was that he had clearly gone from fantasizing to actually planning his kills. He had even detailed the specific weaponry he would use to kill each girl. "Just thinking of killing a lot of young girls makes me happy," he wrote.

When Massey's mother discovered the notebooks, she brought him to Dr. Kenneth Dekelva, a state psychiatrist. Dekelva determined that Jason Massey was a danger to others, diagnosed him with antisocial personality disorder, and placed him in the Dallas Psychiatric Intensive Care Unit. But after psychiatric exams by several other doctors, they couldn't come to a consensus of treatment and eighteen-year-old Jason Massey was released.

After his release, Massey lived with a woman briefly but she kicked him out of her house when she witnessed him killing a dog.

In spring 1993, Massey was pulled over by police. Next to him on the passenger seat was a dead Persian cat with a noose around its neck, a three-pronged knife, and a list of girls' names with check marks next to them. That spring he was briefly detained in jail, where he spent his hours reading about guns and police investigations. He also continued writing in his journals of his plans to commit mass murder. He wrote that he intended, "to grab society by the throat and shake 'em with terror until they're awake and realize what's up so they will remember who I am, when and why I came their way."

———

On June 17, 1993, Christopher Nowlin had asked Jason Massey to give him a ride to see his girlfriend, Christina Benjamin. Nowlin was younger than twenty-year-old Massey and didn't own a car. When Jason met Christina, he started flirting with the thirteen-year-old despite her age and the fact that she was Christopher's girlfriend.

The three of them talked about sneaking out of their parents' house and the idea excited Christina. Christina told Jason that she had never done anything like that but would like to someday. By the end of the night, Jason and Christina had made plans. He told her that he would show up at her house late one night, honk twice, and he would take her out.

That night, Jason and Christopher dropped Christina back at home. On the drive home, Jason told Christopher of his real feelings towards his girlfriend. He told him that he would like to have sex with her, kill her, and cut her up. Not necessarily in that order. Christopher Nowlin would later testify that, at the time, he thought nothing of Massey's disgusting remarks. He told the court that Massy was weird and was always talking about killing girls.

———

July 27, 1993 was hot and humid enough for James King and his wife, Donna Benjamin, to sleep with their bedroom window open. Around 2:00 A.M. James awoke to two short beeps of a car horn in front of their house. His son, fourteen-year-old Brian King, had spent the night in the front yard sleeping on a hammock hung between two trees. When James went to the window, he saw Brian talking to someone in a tan Subaru parked in front of their house. James went to the bathroom and came back to the window a few minutes later, but the car and his son were gone. He stayed awake for another hour and waited for his son to return but, when he didn't return, he went back to bed.

Brian King, Christina Benjamin & Jason Massey

The next morning, James and Donna realized that Brian was still not home. However, they were even more surprised when they noticed Donna's daughter, Christina Benjamin, was missing, too. The kids had never snuck out in the middle of the night before. Although they were worried, James and Donna decided to give them some time to return home. When Brian and Christina hadn't returned by late afternoon, however, they reported the children missing.

———

Two days later, a road worker in Telco, Texas, noticed something in the thick bushes near an old wooden bridge on an extremely rural section of road. The butchered remains of a nude young girl with her head and hands missing were found decomposing in the summer sun. As police searched for the missing body parts, they found another body. Just under the bridge was the body of a young boy.

Using a library card in the boy's pocket, authorities identified the boy as Brian King. Using hair that had caught on a nearby barbed-wire fence and foot x-rays, the girl was identified as Brian's step-sister, Christina Benjamin. Brian King was fully clothed and had been shot twice in the head at close range with a .22 caliber pistol. Christina's injuries were much more sinister. It was obvious that she had been killed by someone with an extreme rage.

Christina's head had been severed at the neck and her hands were cut off at the wrists. The hands and head were never found. She had been shot once in the back and, from bullet fragments on her neck, the medical examiner could tell she had also been shot in the head as well. The shot to the head had most likely ended her life. After death, her abdomen had been cut from her pelvis to her breast. The cut was so deep that some of her internal organs had been exposed and pulled out of her chest cavity. Her genitalia had been carved with delicate precision and both nipples had been cut completely off. Despite the damage to her genitals and breasts, forensic analysis revealed that the girl had not been sexually assaulted.

Physical evidence at the scene was limited. Investigators found a single long, blonde hair on one of Brian King's pant legs that didn't belong to either himself or Christina, as well as a tiny tan colored carpet fiber stuck to the bottom of one of Brian's tennis shoes. From bullet fragments in the bodies, they were able to tell that the bullets were .22 caliber in size.

After identifying the victims, detectives spoke to the friends and family of Brian and Christina. Several friends told police that they had known that Brian and Christina had planned on sneaking out that night with an older boy named Jason. Not long after questioning the friends, police received an anonymous phone call informing them that they need to look into a boy named Jason Massey.

Friends of Jason Massey told detectives that Jason often talked about his obsession with killing animals. Although they had never seen it, Jason had often claimed that he kept a metal cooler in the woods with the skulls of the animals he had killed.

———

In the days after the murders, the owner of a local car wash saw Jason Massey pull into his car wash at 11:30 P.M. and dump some items into the trash. The car then began to back out but, when Massey noticed that he was being watched, he pulled back into the bay and began vacuuming the car. It wasn't until after the car was gone that the owner recognized Jason Massey from the newspaper and notified police.

When detectives sifted through the trash bin and vacuum filter, they found a business card for Massey's probation officer and a red bandana with several blonde hairs on it. The hairs were later matched to Christina Benjamin. They also found a Kentucky Fried Chicken payroll stub with Massey's name on it.

Jason Massey was brought in for questioning and denied any involvement in the crimes. Although he had written in his journals that he had made preparations to evade police, the clues he left were obvious. A search warrant was issued for his home and his tan four-door Subaru.

Massey had stolen a .22 caliber pistol from his cousin and showed the gun to many of his friends in the days before the murders. When police searched his home, they found a Walmart receipt that showed he had purchased ammunition for the handgun, handcuffs, and two hunting knives. After his arrest, the Walmart employee that had sold him the items picked him out of a line-up.

Despite cleaning his Subaru, there was blood all over the inside of his car. Spots were found on the steering wheel, center console, side-step, and passenger seat, as well as a knife in the glove box. In the trunk was a roll of duct tape, tissue paper, electrical tape, a screwdriver, a wrench, a shirt, a jacket, and the head of a hammer. All items tested positive for human blood and were a DNA match for Christina's genetic markers.

Massey was arrested and charged with capital murder. Although the evidence against him was overwhelming, he still pleaded not guilty.

At trial, the deep-seated anger of Jason Massey came to light. Dr. Dekelva testified regarding his prior psychiatric treatment with Massey. The jury heard of his long history of butchering and decapitation of animals and the lists of young girls he intended on killing.

Just before the trial had concluded, a hunter discovered Massey's red metal ice chest in the woods. Inside the cooler were the rotted skulls of thirty-one animals he had decapitated and the four volumes of his "Slayer's Book of Death."

Jason Massey was found guilty of capital murder and, just before sentencing, the jury was able to hear the words written in Massey's books. On October 12, 1994, it took the jury only fifteen minutes to decide that Jason Massey would receive the death penalty.

For the next eight years, Massey unsuccessfully went through the appeals process and turned to Christianity. On April 3, 2001, he was put to death by lethal injection while the relatives of Brian King and Christina Benjamin watched.

Jason Massey's final statement before his death was:

"I would like to speak to the victim's families. First of all, I would like to say that I do not know any of y'all and that is unfortunate, because I would like to apologize to each and every one of you individually. I can't imagine what I've taken from y'all, but I do want to apologize to you for what I did and I want you to know that it was only I that committed the murders. No one else was involved. Christina felt no pain. I swear the things done to her occurred after her death. Her head and hands I threw into the Trinity River. I didn't rape or torture her, either. I admit my guilt and I ask your forgiveness. I pray you will forgive me. If not now, then in the future. May God be with you and keep you through this.

God has used this to change my life. Tonight I dance on the streets of gold. Let those without sin cast the first stone. His servant, Jason Eric Massey."

Investigators, however, thought Massey was lying when he said he threw Christina's head and hands into the Trinity River. They believed Massey had buried them somewhere in hopes that he would someday be released and could return to them for some sort of sadistic sexual pleasure.

5

THE KILLER CLOWN

Marlene Ahrens was just nineteen years old when she found herself divorced with two young boys to raise on her own, both barely out of diapers. When she met Michael Warren, she knew that solitude would change. She knew it was a love that would last.

In April 1972, at just twenty years old, she married again. Her sons, Johnny and Joey Ahrens, kept their biological father's surname but grew up thinking of Michael Warren as their father. Although he was only eighteen when they married, Michael was a smart young man who had the gift of gab. When he spoke, he had the ability to win people over and could sell anything to anyone. Despite being young, Michael had epic hopes and dreams and Marlene knew he was destined for greatness.

Throughout the 1970s Marlene and Michael both grew into savvy entrepreneurs, buying several multi-unit rental properties and collecting rent from their tenants. While Marlene ran the day-to-day operations of the rental properties, Michael opened a used car business called Bargain Motors.

Bargain Motors specialized in well-worn cars and catered to buyers with bad credit that had trouble getting approved for financing at other dealerships. Most of their clientele either had bad credit or had filed for bankruptcy. Bargain Motors would happily finance their cars at exorbitant interest rates. When many of the buyers inevitably missed their payments, Michael hired people to repossess those cars. The cars would then go back on the lot to be sold to other buyers, starting the cycle over again.

Michael, however, liked to cut corners. He was charged with a felony and spent a brief time in jail when he was caught rolling back odometers on his cars so he could sell them at a better price.

Although he could still work in the industry, the felony conviction restricted him from owning a car dealership. To circumvent this, they placed ownership of Bargain Motors into Marlene's name.

In the big picture, the felony conviction was just a speed bump on their financial journey. The property values had increased on their rentals and Bargain Motors grew and expanded into car rentals. The young couple that started with almost nothing had now amassed a net worth of well over $1 million. In 1987, Marlene and Michael purchased a new home in the affluent village of Wellington, Florida, just west of West Palm Beach.

Their new home was in the Aero Club, a private aeronautical housing development with 248 luxurious homes that each sat on one-acre plots of land. Every home came equipped with a private airplane hangar in the backyard and access to a private 4,000-foot lighted runway kept exclusively for the residents.

Life was far from perfect for the family, though. Just after moving into their new home, Marlene's eighteen-year-old son, Joe, had been arrested for aggravated assault. His sentence was light, however, and he served only six months of house arrest. Then tragedy struck. In 1988, Marlene's eldest son, Johnny, died in a car crash. It devastated the entire family. To make matters worse, the relationship between Marlene and Michael was breaking down.

———

It was no secret among the employees of Bargain Motors that Michael had been sleeping around. He often wined and dined women at the Department of Motor Vehicles, working his charm and charisma, hoping to get car title paperwork expedited or altered in his favor. His employees only speculated about his relationships with the girls at the DMV, but they knew one thing for sure: he was having an affair with Sheila Keen.

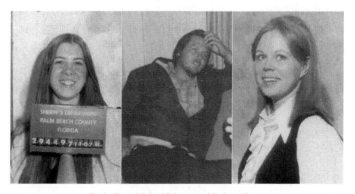

Sheila Keen, Michael Warren & Marlene Ahrens

Sheila Keen and her husband, Richard Keen, ran a business repossessing cars. Michael Warren was one of their biggest clients. Twenty-six-year-old Sheila had long, straight, brown hair and a tough exterior. She was fearless. She had to be to repossess cars. People had a tendency to get angry and violent when their car was being repossessed, so Sheila regularly carried a gun with her everywhere she went.

Sheila had married Richard Keen just three months before she gave birth to their son in 1987. Richard was twenty years older than Sheila and a former leader of the Ku Klux Klan who had spent time in prison for marijuana trafficking.

By 1990, Sheila and Richard had separated but still ran their repo business together. Michael Warren, however, was paying for an apartment for Sheila to live in. Almost every day she showed up at Bargain Motors and she and Michael would leave for lunch together. It was no secret to his employees what was really going on and, eventually, it was no secret to Marlene, either.

In April 1990 Marlene had shared with her mother that she planned on leaving Michael. She was worried about a divorce, however, knowing that after eighteen years of marriage, it would be messy. Their finances were delicately intertwined. Almost all of their assets, including Bargain Motors, were entirely in her name. Marlene told her mother, "If anything ever happens to me… Michael did it."

———

On a rainy Saturday morning during the Memorial Day weekend, Marlene, Joe, and Joe's girlfriend, Jean Pratt, were preparing for breakfast at their home in the Aero Club. Joe had recently broken a bone and sat at the kitchen table with a cast on his leg while Jean made blueberry pancakes. Just before 11:00 A.M., the doorbell rang. Marlene answered the door to find a clown standing on the front porch with an orange wig, a round, red, sponge nose, and thick, white face paint with a painted-on smile. The clown was holding two mylar balloons and a basket of flowers.

Marlene stood in the doorway with a smile on her face and said, "Oh how pretty!" and reached out for the flowers. She had assumed the flowers and balloons were a gift from Michael, who was with friends on their way to the horse races. But it wasn't a gift at all. As Marlene took the flower basket and balloons, the clown pulled out a handgun and shot Marlene in the face.

At first Joe and Jean thought that one of the balloons had popped, but when Marlene fell to the ground, they knew it was a gunshot. Joe ran to his mother as quick as his broken leg would allow him while the clown calmly walked back to the car, still running in the circular driveway.

Marlene was alive but she needed help fast. Joe yelled to Jean to call 911 as he held his mother. Wanting to catch the killer, Joe hobbled toward the car, but it was already pulling out of the driveway. Joe ran back into the house as fast as he could, spoke to the 911 operator for a second, then handed the phone back to Jean. He wanted to unmask the person who was responsible for shooting his mother.

Joe got into his car and drove out of the neighborhood but couldn't catch up to the car. He had spent his entire life around cars and knew that the car was a white convertible Chrysler LeBaron. He also noticed two important details. For one, the clown wasn't wearing typical clown shoes but instead was wearing black boots. He also noticed the one thing that the clown couldn't hide with the makeup and outfit: their eyes. The clown had brown eyes behind all that makeup.

By the time paramedics and police had arrived, Marlene was unconscious but still alive. The single bullet had entered just above her lip, pierced her jaw, and lodged in her spinal cord at the base of her skull. Emergency crews rushed her to the hospital in critical condition.

Joe was able to give police a description of the car but being dressed as a clown made it difficult to describe the assailant. The only things he knew for sure were that the clown had brown eyes and black boots.

The only other clues at the scene were the flowers and mylar balloons that the clown had left behind. The red and white carnations were in a brown wicker basket and the two balloons were imprinted. One said, "You're the Greatest!" while the other had an image of Snow White and the Seven Dwarves.

Within three hours of the shooting, the Palm Beach Sheriff's Office received an anonymous phone call. A female caller told police that they needed to look closely at Marlene's husband, Michael Warren. Michael, however, had an air-tight alibi. He was driving south on the freeway with three of his friends at the time of the shooting, on their way to the horse races.

––––––

While Marlene clung to life, detectives started their investigation by checking flower shops, supermarkets, and costume shops. An important clue came from a local costume shop.

Two days earlier, two women that ran a costume shop had just closed the store for the evening when there was a knock at the door. The costume shop owners explained to the woman with long, straight, brown hair that they were closed for the night, but the woman was desperate. She told the owners that she urgently needed a clown costume. The women let her into the store and she purchased a clown outfit, a bright orange wig, a red sponge nose, and clown makeup. The woman had also requested extra face whitener, stating that she wanted "complete facial coverage."

While investigating the flowers and balloons, detectives learned that the Snow White balloon was a special design. Only one store in the area carried that particular balloon: a Publix supermarket. An employee of the supermarket told police that they had sold the flowers and the two balloons just ninety minutes before the shooting. The employee described virtually the same woman that the costume shop owners had described. A woman with long, straight, brown hair who paid in cash with a $100 bill. The employee also noted that, oddly, the woman wore gloves during the transaction despite the warm Florida weather.

Two days after the shooting, Marlene died in the hospital and the crime was classified as a homicide. Police questioned Michael Warren but it was obvious he hadn't pulled the trigger. He was nowhere near the home at the time of the shooting. However, police wanted to find out if he knew of anyone who would want his wife killed. When questioned, the only idea he had was that the killer could have been a tenant in one of their rental properties. Michael told detectives that he had handled the car business but Marlene dealt with all the properties, which occasionally included evicting tenants that couldn't pay their rent. He suggested that detectives look into some of their former tenants.

Investigators, however, didn't think Michael's hunch was a viable lead. They did what they knew best and followed the evidence. The evidence, so far, had pointed to a woman with long, straight, brown hair and brown eyes. And after speaking to Marlene's family and Michael's employees, the obvious suspect was Sheila Keen.

Several of Michael's employees told detectives that it was common knowledge at the car dealership that Michael and Sheila were having an affair, but both Michael and Sheila denied having any sort of relationship other than professional. Police spoke to tenants in Sheila Keen's apartment complex and many of them mentioned seeing Michael there at all hours of the day and night. In fact, he had been there so often, some of her neighbors had assumed he and Sheila were married and he actually lived there.

Detectives returned to the Publix grocery store, which was just a mile from Sheila Keen's home, to speak again with the employee that had sold the balloons and flower basket. When shown a photo line-up that included Sheila Keen, the employee easily picked her out. The same line-up was shown to the two women at the costume shop. Again, they identified Sheila Keen as the woman that had purchased the clown outfit. Police were sure that the killer was Sheila Keen but they needed more than just circumstantial evidence.

Four days after the murder, the Chrysler LeBaron that the clown had driven was found abandoned in a Winn-Dixie supermarket parking lot eight miles from the crime scene. Forensic investigators examined the car and found orange fibers that were consistent with a clown wig and a long brown hair with the root attached. Within hours of the discovery, detectives had a warrant to search Sheila Keen's apartment.

Inside Sheila Keen's apartment, investigators found a hair in the bathroom trash and orange fibers that were consistent with a clown wig. When criminologists analyzed the hair and fibers, however, they were determined to only be "similar." Not exact. DNA was in its infancy at the time and prosecutors believed the evidence they had was still not enough to put in front of a jury.

When police looked into the background of the Chrysler LeBaron, they found that it was owned by Payless Auto Rentals but had been reported stolen just weeks before the murder. The manner in which it was stolen, however, linked back to Michael Warren's company, Bargain Motors.

Tourists from New York had rented the car from Payless Auto Rental but the car lot was closed when they tried to return it. The couple looked in the phone book and found an ad that used the word "Payless" in large letters at the top of the ad. It was actually an ad for Bargain Motors. It was very similar to the Payless Auto Rental's ad and the tourists mistakenly called Bargain Motors.

The employee that answered the phone at Bargain Motors didn't let the tourists know they were calling the wrong company. Instead, the Bargain Motors employee told the couple to just leave the car parked on the street with the door unlocked and the keys hidden in the sun visor. The tourists did as they were instructed and by morning the car had been stolen.

Detectives believed that Sheila Keen had killed Marlene Warren and that Michael Warren was somehow involved, but they needed a way to prove their theory. To find more evidence, they looked into the background of both Sheila Keen and Michael Warren.

Armed with a warrant, investigators searched Bargain Motors and questioned employees, many of which were relatives of Michael Warren. Although Michael and Sheila adamantly denied having an affair, almost all of his employees told police that the affair was common knowledge. However, rather than finding evidence linking him to the murder, they found evidence of widespread fraud throughout his car business.

Michael Warren and two additional employees of Bargain Motors were arrested. Warren was charged with thirteen felony charges, including racketeering, grand theft, insurance fraud, and operating a chop shop. Although he admitted nothing, employees of Bargain Motors admitted to police that they schemed to steal their own cars, claim insurance on them, and then sell them for parts. They also altered the odometers of many of their cars so they could sell them with lower mileage. It was the same scam that Michael had been arrested for years before. An employee of the Florida Department of Motor Vehicles was also arrested for falsifying title documents for Bargain Motors.

Michael Warren was released on bail but complained to the media that the charges were a sham. He claimed he was being targeted and harassed by the police in retaliation for not cooperating with the investigation of his wife's murder.

In August 1992, Michael Warren was convicted of one count of racketeering, twenty-one counts of odometer fraud, eleven counts of grand theft, and ten counts of petty theft. The racketeering conviction alone carried a maximum sentence of thirty years. With all forty-three felony convictions, Warren faced a potential of 237 years in prison. He got off light and was sentenced to only nine years in prison, then served less than four.

———

When Michael Warren was released from prison in 1998, the murder case of Marlene Warren had gone cold. Although investigators were certain that Sheila Keen was the shooter and believed Michael Warren was involved in some way, they just didn't have the evidence to back up their claim. By 2000, Sheila Keen had divorced her husband Richard and moved from Florida. Michael Warren had been released from prison, Bargain Motors was closed, and he had left Florida as well. The case still haunted investigators, but with the passage of time, they lost track of both their potential suspects.

––––––

In 2014, twenty-four years after the murder, the Palm Beach Sheriff's Office received a $125,000 federal grant to reopen and look into prior cold cases. The murder case of Marlene Warren was one of the many cases reopened and a fresh set of eyes examined the entire case from top to bottom. Witnesses, friends, employees, and family were re-interviewed. Police managed to track down everyone except for the two main characters: Michael Warren and Sheila Keen. However, eventually interviews with Michael Warren's relatives revealed an important piece of information: Michael Warren and Sheila Keen were now married.

For years after the murder, Michael Warren and Sheila Keen had vehemently denied ever having an affair together, This meant detectives were stunned to find that they had married in Las Vegas in 2002 at the Little White Wedding Chapel. Sheila Keen had also changed her name and now went by "Debbie Warren." The couple had been living in Abingdon, Virginia, for the past fifteen years and operated a popular drive-through burger restaurant called The Purple Cow, just across the state border in Tennessee.

When detectives questioned workers at the Purple Cow, two employees claimed that their employer, who they knew as "Debbie," had confessed something to them after a night of heavy drinking. She told them that years ago, she had dressed as a clown and murdered her husband's former wife. At the time, the employees brushed off her claim, assuming she was just drunk and rambling nonsense. It was too crazy to be true. But years later, the employees would realize there may have been some truth to the story.

DNA technology had come a long way in the past twenty-four years. The orange fibers and brown hairs found in the LeBaron and at Sheila Keen's home were re-examined by the new team of investigators. Twenty-seven years after the murder, investigators were finally certain they had enough evidence to bring Sheila Keen-Warren to trial.

Sheila Keen aka: Debbie Warren & Michael Warren

In September 2017, Sheila Keen-Warren was arrested as she and her husband Michael left their home in Abingdon, Virginia. Although Michael Warren was not arrested, Sheila was charged with first-degree murder and placed in the Palm Beach County Jail to await trial. Although investigators have not announced specifically what the DNA evidence is against her, the State Attorney told the media that Sheila Keen-Warren will face either life in prison or the death penalty. At the time of this writing, she is still awaiting a trial that has been delayed several times due to the COVID-19 pandemic. Her trial is currently set for March 2022.

6

THE EYEBALL KILLER

The neighborhood of Oak Cliff in the southwest corner of Dallas, Texas was one of first neighborhoods of Dallas, with its origins dating back to the 1830s. The area thrived throughout the first half of the twenty-first century and was a nice place to raise a family. By the late 1980s, however, as families abandoned the area for the sprawling suburbs, the neighborhood suffered. The north end of Oak Cliff, near the Star Motel, had become a frequent hangout for street prostitutes, pimps, and drug users. It was common to see young girls turning tricks in cars parked in dark alleys, usually to pay for their next hit of heroin or crack.

It was a rough life for a prostitute during those times. With no way to vet the men that picked them up, it was a regular occurrence for the girls to be beaten and robbed by their potential clients.

In mid-December 1990, in a neighborhood called Cotton Valley just south of Oak Cliff, the body of a woman was found at the dead end of a quiet residential street. Detectives knew it was obviously a dump site. She had been killed else-where. The body was laid out with her arms and legs spread wide and her shirt had been pulled up above her breasts. She was naked below the waist and had a bullet hole in her head. She had been shot at close range, indicating that she most likely knew her killer. Bruising on her head and chest revealed that she had been beaten badly before her death.

One of the first police officers on the scene recognized the woman as thirty-three-year-old Mary Pratt. She was a known prostitute that had worked the streets of Oak Cliff near the Star Motel.

The late 80s and early 90s were a rough time in south Dallas and brutal murders certainly weren't unheard of. However, it wasn't until Mary Pratt's body was examined by the patholo-gist that investigators realized the uniqueness of this case. When Dr. Elizabeth Peacock lifted the eyelid of the dead woman, she was startled to find that her right eyeball was missing. Initially, she thought that the eye may have been destroyed by the bullet the woman took to the skull, but when she lifted the left eyelid, she realized that both eyes were missing.

Mary Pratt's eyeballs had not been dug out violently in a fit of anger with disregard to the surrounding skin. There wasn't a scratch on the eyelids. If Dr. Peacock hadn't opened them, she would have had no idea the eyes were even miss-ing. Someone hadn't simply scooped out the eyes, the killer had meticulously removed them and cut the six muscles that hold them in with surgical precision.

———

John Matthews and Regina Smith were police officers assigned to patrol the streets of Oak Cliff near Jefferson Boulevard and the Star Motel. Regina was a thirty-one-year-old rookie cop and sympathized with the young girls selling their bodies. She often talked to them in a feeble attempt to get them off the street and into a better life, but it was a thankless job as most of the girls were so strung out on drugs that they were beyond help.

On December 17, 1990, just days after Mary Pratt's murder, Regina Smith encountered a young prostitute named Veronica Rodriquez. She knew Veronica and had talked to her several times in the past, but this time she looked particularly disheveled. Her face was scratched in several places and she had dried dirt in her hair. Veronica told Officer Smith that she and Mary Pratt had been "doing a double," meaning a man had hired both of them for sex.

Veronica claimed that she and Mary Pratt were attacked but she was able to escape. She said that she ran from the scene and was rescued by a truck driver but she didn't know his name. She told Regina that the attacker was white but "sorta looked Mexican." She said he had salt and pepper hair and a muscular build. At the time, Veronica's description wasn't much help. She was a chronic drug abuser and known for her elaborate, scrambled stories. She couldn't seem to keep her stories straight. Sometimes she claimed that she had seen Mary being shot, other times she hadn't.

———

Two months after the killing, another body was found just a few blocks from where Mary Pratt had been dumped. Again, the victim was a white female, partially nude, her arms and legs spread, and shot in the chest, stomach, and head. And like Mary Pratt, the medical examiner again noticed that both eyes had been meticulously removed without damage to the eyelids or surrounding skin. Someone knew what they were doing and police suspected it was the work of a doctor or surgeon.

Using her fingerprints, the victim was identified as twenty-seven-year-old Susan Peterson. Regina Smith, the beat cop that worked the Oak Cliff streets, knew her. She had also worked near the Star Motel as a prostitute. She had recently spoken of leaving the profession, getting off the street, off of drugs, and getting married. But some sadistic maniac had put an end to that dream.

Police called the two cases a "repeater" but there was no hiding what that really meant—there was a serial killer on the loose in south Dallas.

Officers Smith and Matthews spent the next several weeks warning the street girls of Oak Cliff. They put up flyers near the Star motel and spoke to many of the prostitutes in person. Although they omitted the details of the missing eyeballs, rumors spread and panic ensued throughout the city.

Shortly after the second murder, they ran into Veronica Rodriquez again. This time, they caught her with one of her clients in his car. But when Veronica saw it was Officer Smith, she said, "Don't arrest him! He's the one that saved me!"

The man in the car was Axton Schindler. He worked as a truck driver and, according to his driver's license, lived at 1035 Eldorado Avenue in the north end of Oak cliff, not far from where the two bodies were found.

Officers Smith and Matthews weren't involved in homicide investigations. They were beat cops. They contacted the Homicide detectives handling the case and Axton Schindler was questioned, but there was no evidence against him and no reason to hold him. He was only a person of interest.

———

Some of the black prostitutes in the area assumed that, since the killer had only murdered white women, they were safe. But another body was found just one month after Susan Peterson was killed.

This time, the killer had changed course. The victim was a black female and the body had been dumped about nine miles south of the previous two victims. She was found naked and propped up against a curb on a suburban street. Young children witnessed her body as they walked to the elementary school just a half block away. She was naked and an unopened condom package had been thrown next to her body.

Like the other two, her eyeballs had been removed. However, it seemed that this time the girl had struggled with her killer. She had cuts around her eyes and scratches on her face. Defensive wounds. Although there were no witnesses, fingerprints, or a murder weapon, the medical examiner found a tiny tip of an X-Acto knife embedded in her skull near the eye.

The fact that an X-Acto knife had been used told investigators something important. The murders had not been the work of a doctor or surgeon, as they had suspected—medical professionals didn't use X-Acto knives. The killings had been the work of an amateur with extensive knowledge of anatomy.

The third body was identified as Shirley Williams. She, too, had worked as a prostitute in Oak Cliff but also kept a day job as a housekeeper at the Avalon Motel. She was married and had a young daughter but her family had no idea that she was turning tricks in the evenings. Her body was found naked. However, before she disappeared she had been wearing a yellow raincoat and blue jeans.

Unlike the two prior crime scenes, investigators recovered forensic evidence at the scene of Shirley's murder. Two head hairs were recovered from her left hand and a pubic hair was found on the back of her neck.

———

After the third killing, many prostitutes who had worked the area near the Star Motel left town or found some other way to make money. Many, of course, stayed, as it was their only way of getting money for their next hit of heroin or crack.

Officers Smith and Matthews still did their best to warn girls of the dangerous maniac that was targeting them when they came across a black prostitute named Brenda White.

Brenda told the officers that she had been picked up by a trick and they had agreed to drive to a certain location for their rendezvous. But when he started driving in the opposite direction, she knew something was wrong. She screamed, "let me out!" and then jumped out of the car before the car had even stopped. As she ran away from the car, the man screamed, "I hate whores! I'm gonna kill all of you motherfucking whores!" The man chased after her and just before he was able to get to her, she turned around and maced him in the face.

Brenda White described her attacker as having salt and pepper hair, cowboy boots, and driving a dark station wagon. The "salt and pepper" hair rang a bell with the officers. Although the description didn't match Axton Schindler, it was similar to the one that Veronica Rodriquez had given of her attacker. Although they weren't assigned to the case of the murders, the two cops took it upon themselves to investigate on their own.

With the help of the Dallas county deputy constable, Walter Cook, and the Dallas county computer system, they searched for information on Axton Schindler. When they checked the address that Schindler had listed on his driver's license, the house at 1035 Eldorado came up as being owned by a man named Fred Albright. Nothing was mentioned about Axton Schindler living there. Further searches, however, revealed that Fred Albright owned another property in Cotton Valley, very close to where the first two bodies were found. Yet another search revealed that Fred Albright was actually dead.

Walter Cook recognized the surname Albright. He had handled a case just a few weeks prior in which a woman that had been a friend of Mary Pratt had dated a man named Charles Albright. The woman had claimed that Albright was a very nice man but had become increasingly violent and had a strange fascination with eyes. She had also mentioned noticing X-Acto knives in his home.

When the three officers typed in the name Charles Albright, they found that he was fifty-seven years old and had a police record, including miscellaneous charges of theft, forgery, burglary, and molestation of a child. He had briefly served time in prison, had salt and pepper gray hair, and his address was listed as 1035 Eldorado.

Charles Albright

When they saw that his mugshot from the most recent arrest matched Brenda White's description, they contacted the Homicide detectives handling the murder cases.

Charles Albright's photo was put in a photo lineup with several other mugshots. Both Brenda White and Veronica Rodrigues definitively pointed him out as their attacker. Detectives knew they had their killer.

———

Charles Albright was adopted just three weeks after his birth by Delle and Fred Albright. Although Delle Albright pampered her son, she was also overbearing, overprotective, and sometimes cruel. When he wouldn't take a nap, Delle would tie him to his bed. When he had done something wrong, she would lock him in a dark room. Worried that he might contract diseases, she bathed him and changed his clothes several times a day. On some occasions, she dressed him in girl's clothing and let him play with dolls. The education of her son was very important to Delle. Although Charles went to normal public schools, she homeschooled him as well, and he was bumped two grades ahead in his early school years. During his grade school years, Delle made sure Charles practiced playing piano for thirty minutes every morning before the school bus arrived.

Charles's mother taught him manners and to be kind, especially when it came to girls. Throughout his life, there was no shortage of people that had extremely good things to say about Charles Albright. He was known to be a perfect gentleman around women, even in his adult years.

When Charles was eleven-years-old, Delle ordered a taxidermy kit for him through the mail. It was a hobby that had interested her in her early years and she wanted to teach it to Charles. He took on his new hobby as an art form, learning how to properly skin birds and small animals, as well as how to remove brains, organs, and, of course, eyeballs.

When Charles's mother took him to taxidermy shops, he was fascinated by the intricate fake eyeballs. He could stare at them for hours. Delle, however, wouldn't allow him to buy the eyes. They were far too expensive. Instead, she would sew black buttons onto his projects instead of letting him use the more realistic eyes.

Delle displayed her son's creative artwork in the cabinets of their home. The birds were stuffed perfectly except for their large, black button eyes.

As Charles grew up, he excelled academically and graduated from high school at fifteen. But he was a prankster. He set fire to his high school chemistry teacher's dress and was caught stealing the answers to tests while in college. When his grades became less than perfect, he learned to forge his report cards so his mother believed he earned all A's.

Gradually, through the years, his juvenile pranks got more and more serious. Eventually, he was breaking into stores and stealing things. During his college years, he and several of his classmates were caught during a break-in and he was sentenced to a year in prison.

After prison, he attended Arkansas State Teacher's College and excelled in science and human anatomy, then planned to continue on to medical school to become a surgeon.

By the time Charles Albright was thirty-six, he had taken a job teaching science in a small town just outside of Dallas. To get the job, he presented the school with paperwork that showed he had a master's degree in biology from East Texas State University and was working on a second master's in counseling and a Ph.D. in biology. He was a well-liked teacher: clearly intelligent but a bit eccentric. He even coached the football team. But the school eventually learned that all of his credentials had been forged. He didn't even have a bachelor's degree, let alone a master's. Charles pleaded guilty to fraud and was sentenced to one year of probation. Amazingly, he had managed to keep the news from his wife Bettye and their daughter.

Throughout the years, Charles worked dozens of random jobs while his wife taught high school English. Most of his jobs didn't last very long before he moved on to the next one. He collected movie posters, made baseball bats, had hopes of starting his own winery, went to beauty school and became a hair stylist, worked for a company that designed airplanes, and worked as an illustrator, a bullfighter, and an artist painting custom portraits. When he was commissioned to paint a portrait for a friend, he painted a beautiful six-foot by three-foot canvas of his friend's wife. Everything in the portrait was perfect except for the eyes. They were blank. Months later, he finished the portrait and the eyes were perfect. The most realistic part of the painting.

Charles's offenses slowly escalated in severity. In 1971 he was arrested for forging checks, in 1979 he was caught stealing bottles of perfume, and in 1980 he was arrested for stealing from a hardware store. For that, he served six months in prison. Delle Albright couldn't bear having her friends know that her son was in prison and told everyone that he was working at a nuclear power plant in Florida.

In 1985, Charles was active in St. Bernard's Catholic Church. He sang in the choir, helped with Communion, and assisted the priest in any way he could. It was at the church where he met and befriended a family with young children. He gave the kids presents at Christmas time and dressed as Santa. He even bought the family a big box of steaks. Everyone at the church was shocked, however, when one of the family's young girls claimed that Charles had snuck into her bedroom and molested her.

The family and the church couldn't believe it. The man they referred to as "Good Ol' Charlie" had molested a girl. In March 1985, at fifty-one-years old, Charles Albright pleaded guilty to molesting the nine-year-old girl. In exchange for his guilty plea, he was only charged with probation.

Charles's marriage to Bettye ended and, in 1985, he met Dixie Austin. In October 1990, just before the killings started, Charles Albright took a job delivering newspapers for the Dallas Times Herald. The job kept him out in the late-night hours while his new common-law wife slept at home. At fifty-seven-years-old, Charles Albright took up a new hobby that involved prostitutes and eyeballs.

Just after 2:00 A.M. on March 23, 1991, a team of tactical officers threw flashbang grenades into the home at 1035 Eldorado and pulled Charles Albright from the home wearing only his red underwear. Officers Regina Smith and John Matthews, along with detectives from the Homicide division, arrested Albright and charged him with three counts of murder.

Albright's girlfriend, Dixie Austin, stood in shock as her partner was dragged away and officers began their search of the house. The search revealed several X-Acto knives, anatomy books, and true crime books about Edmund Kemper, the Ypsilanti Ripper, Ted Bundy, and the Texas Baby Murders. They also found newspaper clippings about the three murders and several guns hidden in a wall beside the fireplace. Although there were several guns, none of them were a match for the guns that had killed the three victims. And there was no sign of any eyeballs.

Charles Albright also kept a storage unit. The storage unit contained his taxidermy equipment with dozens of formaldehyde-filled jars containing dead frogs and salamanders. Stuffed birds sat on shelves, but still no eyeballs. Again, it was all circumstantial evidence but it showed that he had the ability to remove eyeballs with precision.

Officers Regina Smith and John Matthews took to the streets again to talk to the prostitutes of Oak Cliff. Now that the police had a suspect in the killings, the girls spoke more freely. Over and over again, the women picked him out of a photo lineup. Many said that he was a regular customer and that he was usually very nice and had often purchased them meals, but had strange sexual requests. He like to beat them with a rope.

One prostitute, Tina Connolly, saw his photo and told police that she and Shirley Williams were picked up by him on the night she was murdered. They had driven to a field where he had attacked both of them but Tina was able to escape.

When Tina brought the officers to the field where she had last seen Shirley Williams, they found Shirley's yellow raincoat in a pile of trash. Analysis showed that the coat contained blood spatter but weather had degraded the DNA. Animal hair was found on the coat, which ended up being squirrel hair that matched to squirrel hair collected from Albright's vacuum cleaner bag. The coat also contained eight head hairs that belonged to Shirley Williams. The hairs that were found on Shirley Williams' hand were a match for Charles Albright.

——————

Charles Albright claimed to have never touched an eyeball and denied ever being with prostitutes at all, let alone killing them. But a jury disagreed. Charles Albright was tried only for the murder of Shirley Williams, as that was the case with the most evidence. He was found guilty and sentenced to life in prison.

To this day, many question whether Charles Albright was actually the real Eyeball Killer. The evidence against him was mostly circumstantial and no real evidence linked him to the first two murders. Although Charles claimed he had never met any of the girls and didn't know the names of the motels where they worked, the murders mysteriously stopped after his arrest.

Axton Schindler fled just before Albright's trial and was never seen again. Prosecutors didn't believe he had anything to do with the murders, although he may have known that Albright was the killer.

Charles Albright died at the age of eighty-seven on August 20, 2020, at the West Texas Regional Medical Facility in Lubbock, Texas. He maintained his innocence until his dying day.

7

HORSESHOE LAKE

J ust thirty miles southwest of Memphis, where the Mississippi River divides Arkansas from Tennessee, lies the tiny town of Horseshoe Lake. The lake itself was once just a tight bend of the Mississippi, but an earthquake in 1812 moved the land and shifted the flow of the river. The two ends of the tight bend filled with land and separated the bend from the river, creating an "oxbow lake" which took the shape of a horseshoe. The Mississippi River that had once meandered west, then east, suddenly flowed due south. The newly formed lake became the second largest lake in Arkansas, standing just a few feet from the Mississippi River and aptly named Horseshoe Lake.

In the late 1800s, the Snowden family owned more than 1,000 acres of land on the shores of the lake, where Robert Bogardus Snowden operated a cotton plantation. The family came from money. Robert's grandfather had been a colonel in the Civil War and the family of his grandmother, Anne Brinkley, had built the railroad that spanned 140 miles from Memphis, Tennessee to Little Rock, Arkansas.

The land stayed in the Snowden family for decades and in 1919, Robert and Anne's son, Robert Brinkley Snowden, built a beautiful but modest single-story house on the banks of Horseshoe lake with his wife, Grace. Robert operated a cotton field near the home while Grace raised their four children, Sally, Edie, Dorothy, and Robert. The children enjoyed their early years living on the lake until they were later sent to Memphis for school.

In 1949, the beautiful but unassuming single-story house went through a massive transformation. The house was renovated into a luxurious three-story, 6,000 square foot mansion with a large porch, sweeping staircase, crystal chandelier, and marble flooring. The family dubbed it Snowden House, which was built in the style of a colonial Antebellum mansion more commonly found in Louisiana. Through the decades, it was home to several members of the Snowden family who also operated thirty rental cabins that they owned along the lakeside.

Sally Snowden, one of the daughters, had moved away from the area after she finished school and married an actor from New York, David McKay. The couple had children and lived in San Francisco but eventually divorced in 1976. By then, their children were grown and Sally moved back to Horseshoe Lake to start her own accounting firm in Memphis.

Sally loved the area around Horseshoe Lake and had fond memories of spending her childhood there with her siblings. By 1982, her mother and father had both passed away, leaving the family corporation to be divided equally among the four children and their children. With her background in accounting, the Snowden family put Sally in charge of managing the business, which included Snowden House and the rental properties surrounding the lake.

Snowden House evolved into a beautiful bed-and-breakfast and occasional event space. It was used as a filming location for the John Grisham movie The Client with Susan Sarandon and Tommy Lee Jones. The family also leased properties in the area, which included the thirty lakefront cabins, farmland, industrial properties, an orchard, and a fishing camp. Sally lived in a house that she owned on the lake near Snowden House and also ran a small antique store in the area.

Several other descendants of the original Snowden family lived along the banks of the lake, including Sally's nephew, Joseph "Lee" Baker. He, his wife Carol, and their three sons lived in a home near Snowden House. Lee Baker started playing guitar in his early teens, in the 1960s, and by 1996 was a sought-after guitarist in the Memphis blues scene. Lee played with a diverse range of artists including Charlie Rich, Mississippi Fred McDowell, Iggy Pop, MC5, Alex Chilton, and Big Star.

Although he was a popular guitarist, music didn't pay the bills—which meant Lee also taught English at the nearby Hughes High School. But his true love was his music. He had worked incessantly at his music career for almost thirty years and developed a devoted following. In 1996, his own band, Lee Baker and the Agitators, were days away from recording their own record. Rather than deal with a record label, however, Lee had saved large amounts of cash so the band could press and promote their own record.

In August 1996, tragedy struck when the Bakers' home on Horseshoe Lake was destroyed by a fire. Luckily, none of the family members were home at the time, but the damage to the house was extreme. It was a complete loss. Lee Baker lost an irreplaceable guitar collection and all the cash that he had saved for the band's record pressing. The fire had been so intense that it bubbled the paint on the side of a firetruck that came to douse the flames. After analyzing the debris, the Fire Marshall determined that the fire had been intentionally set. It was arson. Someone had set the house on fire to destroy evidence of a robbery.

The Baker family was devastated by the loss. After their home was destroyed, Lee Baker and his family temporarily moved into one of the Snowden cabins on the lake, just steps away from his aunt Sally's home.

In addition to his music career and teaching English at the local high school, Lee helped Sally run the family business. On a Tuesday morning, just one month after the fire, Lee left their temporary home and drove his truck to Sally's house to help with the bookkeeping. It was early in the month and Lee had just collected the rent payments for many of the leased properties. Sally and Lee had planned on doing the books and making the deposit for the month.

———

Later that morning, a local man, Bobby Couples, saw a red Toyota Camry crashed on the side of the road. The car had hit a tree and rolled on its side with the engine still running. The windshield had been shattered. It looked as if someone had hit their head on the windshield during the crash. But when Bobby peered inside the car, there was nobody inside.

Bobby drove to a nearby boat shop where his friend, Levi Glasper, worked. The two men drove back to the car and Levi instantly recognized it. It belonged to Sally Snowden McKay.

Levi and Bobby drove to Sally's home and found that Lee Baker's white GMC Sierra truck was backed up tightly against the back door of the home. It was parked so close to the home that they couldn't get in through the door. When they tried the front door, it was locked. Levi, however, knew something was wrong when he tried to look inside one of the windows and noticed that the glass was hot to the touch. They quickly drove back to the boat shop to call the fire department.

While waiting for the fire department to arrive, Levi and Bobby used a tow winch to pull Lee Baker's truck away from the door. Although the fire had not reached the outside of the house, once inside, firefighters discovered that the kitchen and living room were ablaze.

The fire was quickly contained and the damage was minimal. Like the home of the Baker family, the cause of the fire was arson. This time, however, the fire was set to hide not only a robbery but also to hide two murders.

Inside the house, emergency crews found the bodies of seventy-five-year-old Sally Snowden McKay and her nephew, fifty-three-year-old Lee Baker. The bodies had been badly burned, but they had not died from the fire or smoke inhalation. Both Lee and Sally had been shot.

————

As police investigated the scene, they found that the cash that Lee had collected in rent was missing. The house that Lee had been temporarily living in was robbed as well. Although they found no shell casings at the scene, they were able to collect fingerprints and palm prints from the passenger side of the Toyota Camry, as well as hair samples from the car's headliner. Police believed that whoever crashed the car had hit their head on the windshield and then crawled out of the passenger side window while the car was on its side.

Police questioned a nearby resident who claimed to have recognized Sally's car being driven recklessly down the street by two young black men. One young man, who had a criminal past and lived nearby, was twenty-year-old Edrick Lewis. Edrick had grown up just a few doors down from Lee Baker and played with Lee's sons his entire life. Police brought him in for questioning and took fingerprints and hair samples. They also gave him a polygraph, which he passed. However, when they checked with Edrick's parole officer, they found that he was actually with his parole officer in another city several miles away when the murders happened. He couldn't have been involved.

Lee Baker's son, Joe, however, had an idea of who might have been involved. Joe had grown up with Edrick's younger brother, Travis. Joe had noticed that fifteen-year-old Travis Lewis had recently begun to hang out with the wrong kids, doing drugs, and changing his ways. Joe told detectives that he believed Travis had robbed the homes, started the fires, and could have been involved in the murders as well.

Joe explained that Travis had recently stolen a video game from him and his father, Lee, had confronted Travis about it. Just a year earlier, Travis had stolen a check from Sally Snowden McKay and tried to cash it. Stealing a video game and cashing a bad check, however, were a long stretch from double homicide. Although detectives had a hard time imagining that a fifteen-year-old boy could have been involved in such a heinous crime, they brought him in for questioning.

Travis Lewis & Snowden House

Police interrogated the boy without his parents present. During the questioning, Travis denied any involvement in either of the fires or the murders. He claimed that he was at home on the day of the murders and watched the firetrucks speed toward Sally's house from his front porch.

Travis attended Hughes High School, the same school where Lee Baker taught English. The school verified that Travis was not in attendance that day—he had been suspended. Travis was given three polygraph tests, all of which he passed. Police then took hair samples and let him go for the time being.

Over the next two weeks, detectives analyzed the evidence that had been collected. When the fingerprints from the Camry matched those of Travis Lewis, they brought him in for a fourth polygraph. This time, he failed.

After failing the fourth polygraph, Travis changed his story. He told police that early on the morning of the killings, his mother thought he had left to ride his bike to school. But instead he was riding his bike to Lee Baker's temporary house, intent on breaking in and stealing whatever he could find. On his way, he ran into his friend, Andre, who was skipping school that day and wanted to break into the house with him. But Andre had a better idea—he suggested that Travis break into the Bakers' home while Andre break into Sally Snowden McKay's home.

Travis claimed that he was rummaging through the Bakers' home, looking for things to steal, when Andre showed up driving Sally's red Toyota Camry. "Get in," he said. "I just killed some folks and I need to get rid of the bodies."

According to Travis, his friend Andre had a Colt .25 automatic pistol with him and killed Lee and Sally when they caught him trying to break in. Afterwards, he threw the pistol into Horseshoe Lake. Travis insisted he was nowhere near the house when they were killed.

Andre and Travis drove back to Sally's house, but the bodies were too heavy for the young boys to move. Andre placed sheets over the bodies, doused them in gasoline, and lit them on fire. They then left the house and backed Lee's truck against the back door so the fire would destroy any evidence before firefighters could get in to put it out.

With Andre driving, they sped through the neighborhood in Sally's car but hit a tree and rolled the car onto its side. That was when Travis left his fingerprints and bits of his hair inside the car as he climbed out. Given his confession, Travis Lewis was arrested for the robbery.

———

Detectives found that Travis' friend Andre had checked into a nearby hospital just after the murders using an assumed name. He had knocked one of his teeth out during in the car crash. When police questioned Andre, however, he claimed that he wasn't anywhere near Horseshoe Lake that day. He said he was with his girlfriend the entire time and his girlfriend backed up his story.

Although police took fingerprints, as well as hair and DNA samples, from Andre, none of them matched anything from the car or crime scene. Every piece of evidence, however, matched Travis, so prosecutors changed the charges against Travis. In addition to the robbery charge, Travis Lewis was charged with two counts of capital murder.

At just fifteen, Travis was to be tried as an adult. In Arkansas, a capital murder conviction had only two possible sentences: life in prison without the possibility of parole or the death penalty.

Just days before the capital murder trial of Travis Lewis was to begin, prosecutors offered him a deal. He was offered a lighter sentence in exchange for a guilty plea. If he took the deal, someday he might actually be able to get out of jail. Travis's lawyer knew that a black man charged with the murder of two white people in Arkansas with an almost all-white jury stood almost no chance of success. Travis Lewis accepted the plea deal, avoided a trial, and was sentenced to twenty-eight and a half years in prison for the murders and five years for the burglary. The sentences were to be served concurrently.

———

In the months after the murders, Sally's sister, Edie, took over management of the family corporation but couldn't do it alone. Sally's daughter, Martha McKay, had been living in Seattle, Washington, in the years before her mother's death. She now returned to Memphis to help.

The 1949 remodel of Snowden House had seen fifty years of wear and tear and, inevitably, the bed-and-breakfast had to be closed. Martha had never lived at Snowden House but spent every summer there with her siblings throughout her childhood. She had fond memories of the opulent home and longed to see it restored back to its original southern charm.

Martha had experience restoring homes. After attending the University of Washington, she restored historic properties in both Seattle and Virginia City, Nevada, to the original luster of their time period. During the early 2000s, the real estate market was booming and Martha offered to buy Snowden House from the family with plans to restore it to its historic condition.

Martha spent several years and over $100,000 of her own money doing an extensive renovation of the home. However, when the real estate market took a downturn, she wasn't able to sell it as she'd planned. As an alternative, she turned the once again beautiful home into an event space. Snowden House became a popular venue for weddings and parties. Martha's work on the historic home had been done so well that Memphis Magazine ran a feature article in 2012 about Martha and the extensive restoration.

———

Martha had been a practicing Buddhist most of her adult life and believed wholeheartedly in forgiveness. She made it known to her fellow family members that she didn't hold a grudge against Travis Lewis over the death of her mother. She was sympathetic because the boy was influenced by drugs at such a young age. She also wasn't necessarily convinced that Travis was the one that killed Sally and Lee.

She couldn't believe that the fifteen-year-old could have possibly acted alone, despite his guilty plea.

As the years pressed on, Martha became friends with Travis's mother, Gladys, who still lived in the Horseshoe Lake area, and offered her a job at Snowden House as a housekeeper. The two became good friends and had mutual respect for one another. Deep down, Martha knew that if Travis had just been given a better chance, his life could have been different. She told him so in letters that she wrote to him in prison. Travis wrote back and they exchanged letters several times. She explained that she had faith in him and, in the years to come, she attended his parole hearings to make a case for his release.

Every other member of the Snowden family felt exactly the opposite of Martha. They felt that Travis was where he needed to be—in prison—and he should stay there. The Snowden family showed up at his parole hearings as well, sitting next to Martha but pleading for him to be kept behind bars.

Martha McKay & Travis Lewis

In 2018, however, when Martha and Gladys showed up at Travis's parole hearing, he was finally released from prison. After serving twenty-four years of his sentence, thirty-seven-year-old Travis was a free man. He had lived more of his life behind bars than in the free world. Martha was proud of her choice to help and made good on her promise of support. She gave him a job as a groundskeeper at Snowden House so he could work alongside his mother. For the next year, Travis managed to stay out of trouble and seemed to be doing well for himself. However, in early 2020, things began to change.

Gladys Lewis was the first to notice the change in her son. She warned Martha, "Stay away from Travis. He's going back to his old ways." Prison had not rehabilitated him and Travis had gone back to doing drugs with old friends. Martha, however, wasn't the type to give up easily. She had faith in him—but her faith would only take her so far and she realized that Gladys was right. Martha had sold a crystal chandelier for $10,000 and the cash disappeared before she could deposit it. She knew it was Travis. He was the only person that had seen where she kept the money in the house.

Martha confronted Travis and blamed him for the missing money. She fired him and told him he wasn't welcome in Snowden House ever again.

———

In the early morning of March 25, 2020, Sheriff's deputies responded to an alarm that had been triggered at Snowden House. The deputies entered the house through the back door and announced their presence but no one answered. As they walked through the house, they heard footsteps on the second floor and charged up the stairs.

The deputies climbed the stairs to find a pile of clothes and bedding at the top of the stairs, which seemed to be covered in some sort of liquid. Down the hall, they heard noises and a man's voice on the other side of a closed bathroom door. When they called for the man to come out of the bathroom, however, they heard a loud crash from behind the door.

Through an upstairs window, one of the deputies saw movement outside on the grass below. The man in the bathroom had jumped out of the second-story window, seemingly unharmed. The deputies rushed back down the stairs but, by the time they got out of the house, the man had taken off in a car. But he didn't get far. The car was stuck in mud. The man flung the car door open and sprinted toward the dock on Horseshoe Lake.

The deputies chased the man toward the dock, firing a taser gun at him twice but both shots missing. The man sprinted to the end of the dock and dove into the water. Deputies waited, watching the water, but the man never came back up.

Initially, police believed they had simply interrupted a robbery in progress and assumed nobody other than the robber was in the house. It wasn't until a neighbor pointed out that Martha McKay's car was parked in the garage that they went back into the house to look for her. Underneath the pile of clothes and linens at the top of the stairs was the body of Martha McKay. She had been bludgeoned and stabbed to death. Near the body was a bloody box cutter knife and a bag containing jewelry and other valuables.

The pile of clothing covering her body had been doused in a flammable liquid. It was clear that the killer had intended to set the house on fire to destroy evidence.

Rescue crews used sonar to search Horseshoe Lake throughout the night and located the body of Travis Lewis. He had drowned. An autopsy revealed he had cocaine, methamphetamines, and marijuana in his system.

Twenty-four years after her mother had been killed, Martha McKay was murdered by the same killer that she had helped get out of prison. After 101 years in the Snowden family, Snowden house was sold and demolished.

8

THE CAM GIRL OBSESSION

S ylvia Ventsislavova reapplied her deep red lipstick, adjusted her lacy black bustier, and clicked the green "LIVE" button on her computer screen.

"Good evening, sweetie. How was your day? I've been thinking about you. Dirty thoughts…" she said to her webcam as her perfectly curled hair trickled over her shoulder.

"I guarantee my thoughts were dirtier," Grant replied. "Oh my God, you look so stunning."

Although Grant Amato had never really met "Silvie," who lived in Bulgaria, he considered her his girlfriend. She told him so. And he believed. He loyally logged on to watch the sexy raven-haired beauty do her private webcam show for him every night after work. He absolutely couldn't tell her "no." She was all he thought about.

Sylvia "Silvie" Ventsislavova

Each night, Grant Amato told Silvie about how much money he was making as a professional gamer, the fancy new BMW he drove, and the nice, big house he owned in Florida. She probably didn't believe a word of it. Or maybe she did. After all, he was spending more than $2,000 a night to watch her take off her clothes, tease him with the lingerie he had purchased for her, and use the sex toys he would send her. But Grant's stories were all lies. The truth was, Grant Amato had an amazingly privileged life that he squandered for an online stripper he had never met.

———

Grant Amato and his older brother, Cody, spent their childhood preparing for the future. Grant, Cody, and their adopted brother, Jason, lived with their parents in a beautiful home in Chuluota, Florida, just east of Orlando. Grant and Cody weren't just brothers—they were the best of friends. As children, they both loved the Florida Gators football team, enjoyed fitness, and were on the school weightlifting team.

After high school, Grant and Cody both attended the University of Central Florida and had similar plans for the rest of their lives. They both planned to go to nursing school to study anesthesiology, they would buy matching BMWs, and when their parents retired to Tennessee, together they would buy the family home. The entire Amato family worked in healthcare. Their father, Chad, worked as a Clinical Pharmacist for CVS and their mother, Margaret, worked as a Client Operations Manager for a healthcare company.

But Grant and Cody's plans didn't turn out quite as they had hoped. Grant graduated from nursing school in 2011 with a bachelor's degree in nursing but wasn't quite ready for his master's in anesthesiology. He failed during his first year. While Cody continued on, Grant took a nursing job for AdventHealth Orlando.

Grant, however, ruined his chances of continuing with any job in the medical profession when he was accused of stealing eight vials of Propofol, a drug used to induce anesthesia. It was the same drug that was a key ingredient in the cocktail of drugs that killed Michael Jackson. In the summer of 2018, co-workers believed he was suicidal and accused him of stealing the drug.

His co-workers were correct. On June 21, 2018, Grant Amato was caught with the drug and arrested on charges of grand theft. His brother, Cody, came to his rescue. Cody shelled out $8,000 for an attorney to represent him and the charges were dropped. But his future job prospects were slim.

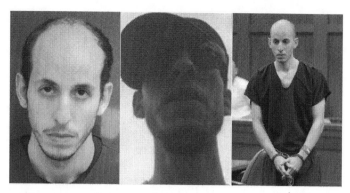

Grant Amato

The generosity of his family saved him at every turn. At twenty-nine years old, Grant moved back in with his parents and spent his time locked in his childhood bedroom playing video games. He believed it would be his new career path. The video game streaming site Twitch had made a few select video gamers tons of money with online gaming; Grant felt that he was good enough to create a new career as a professional gamer.

But like many young men who lock themselves in their bedroom, Grant's eye turned toward porn. Specifically, a website called myfreecams.com where he found an exotic Bulgarian beauty named Silvie. In Grant Amato's mind, virtual reality became reality. When Silvie professed her love for him, nothing else mattered. He believed.

To watch one minute of Silvie's sexy show required 90 digital tokens. Grant purchased bundles of 5,000 tokens at a time for $600. Each night, he watched and chatted with Silvie for roughly four hours, racking up more than $2,500 in charges per night. Without a job, Grant was spending money he didn't have.

When his credit cards were maxed out, Grant needed to find other means to feed his addiction and pay his virtual girlfriend. His brother, Cody, and his father, Chad, both loaned him money under the belief that it would be used to promote his new career as a live-streaming gamer on Twitch. While they had a sinking suspicion he was lying, they had no idea all the money was going to a Bulgarian cam girl.

It didn't take long before the loans from family members ended and Grant Amato was running out of options. Rather than ask for more loans from his father and brother, Grant simply began stealing from them. Within just a few months, he had drained their bank accounts and Silvie was getting rich.

In November 2018, Grant's father and brother realized that Grant had access to their bank accounts and credit cards and had stolen more than $200,000. Rather than press charges, Grant's loving family forgave him once again. Instead of punishing him, they somehow thought an all-expenses-paid trip to Japan with Cody would do him some good. The brothers had always dreamed of taking a trip to Japan together and the family thought now would be the perfect time.

That December, Cody and Grant spent a fun-filled week in Japan. But when they returned to Florida on December 15, it was soon clear that their plan had not worked. Grant was still obsessed with Silvie and would do anything necessary to speak to her again.

On December 19, Grant and his father had a particularly heated argument. Chad had had enough of Grant's nonsense. In a fury, Grant told his parents that he felt worthless and "really tired of everything. I'm just going to handle it my own way" before he stormed out of the house.

That evening, when Grant hadn't returned home, his parents reported him missing, telling police that he had "strong feelings of worthlessness" and they were worried he was having suicidal thoughts again.

Grant took refuge at his aunt's house, thirty miles away in Apopka, Florida. Donna Amato could tell that Grant was troubled and agreed to let him stay at her home temporarily, but she had no idea the level of turmoil that was brewing at his home.

Within days, Donna Amato was at her wit's end. Initially, she thought that her bank account had been hacked—her credit cards had been maxed out. However, when she called the bank only to find out that the charges had happened from within her own household, she was furious. Her nephew was to blame. Grant Amato was at it again.

Chad Amato called his sister and begged her not to press charges against Grant. He told her of the family's problems and their frustration at trying to keep him in line, but they didn't know what to do. It was the first time Donna Amato had ever heard her brother cry when he told her that he had taken a second mortgage on their home and would need to work several more years before he could retire. All just to pay off Grant's credit card debt.

On December 22, the Amato family picked Grant up from his aunt's home, drove him to South Florida, and checked him into a voluntary rehabilitation clinic. The rehab was scheduled to last two months but Grant didn't last long. He checked himself out after only two weeks and, on January 9, returned to the family home.

Chad Amato had heard enough of his son's excuses. If Grant wanted to stay in their home, he would need to agree to their strict terms and conditions. Chad took his son out to dinner and presented him with a contract. The handwritten contract had been drawn up by Cody, Margaret, and Chad and it laid down the rules of the house.

If Grant intended to stay in the family home, he would need to agree to a precise set of rules. Any variance from the rules and he would be out on his own—permanently cut off from the family.

The contract stated that Grant was to get a job. A real job. No more pretending to be a professional gamer. He would have no more access to a cell phone and he was no longer able to spend his nights on the internet. This meant absolutely no contact with Silvie. None. And, most importantly of all, there would be no more financial help from anyone in the family.

Grant, of course, couldn't control himself. Within a week, he had used his mother's cell phone to message Silvie on Twitter. When his father found out that he had violated their contract, Chad grabbed Grant by the shirt collar and commanded that he pack his bags and find his own place to live. Later that morning, Chad and Cody both left for work while Grant packed his bags.

In the late afternoon of January 24, Grant Amato slowly packed his bags and sulked about the situation he had gotten himself into. As he packed his belongings, rather than pack his gun, he pulled it out of its case and quietly walked into the den, where his mother worked at her computer. He put the gun up to the back of his mother's head and pulled the trigger. Margaret Amato slumped over her desk as her blood pooled around her computer keyboard.

Grant Amato then sat for almost an hour in the kitchen and waited for his father to arrive home from work. Although Chad Amato regularly carried a holstered pistol on his hip, he didn't stand a chance when he walked into the house. Grant shot him twice as he entered the kitchen.

With both of his parents dead in the house, Grant Amato waited for more than four hours for his brother to return home from work around 10:00 P.M. He had time to think. Time to consider his actions. Cody Amato had done everything he possibly could to help the brother, who he had loved since the day he was born. Grant repaid that love with a bullet to Cody's head as he walked into the house, still wearing his medical scrubs.

Grant Amato picked up the four shell casings that had been ejected from his own gun and replaced them with shell casings from Cody's gun. He then placed Cody's gun near his body in an attempt to make it seem as if Cody had shot their parents and then killed himself.

Just after midnight, Grant left the house and drove to a Publix grocery store and sat in the parking lot to use their public Wi-Fi. At 2:00 A.M., he logged onto the internet and used Cody's debit card to purchase tokens to speak to Silvie.

———

The next morning, just before 9:00 A.M., a neighbor claimed to have heard what sounded like a gunshot coming from the Amato home. Police had also received a call from Cody's co-workers, who were concerned when he hadn't shown up for work that morning. When police arrived for a routine wellness check at 9:17 A.M. they found the three bodies. Each one was shot execution-style. The blood surrounding each body had already dried, meaning it wasn't possible for them to have been killed anywhere near 9:00 A.M., as the neighbor suggested.

At 10:00 A.M. on January 26, Grant had a job interview with Express Scripts and checked into a nearby Doubletree Hilton hotel in the early afternoon. The following morning, he was arrested in his hotel room.

During questioning, Grant didn't ask why he had been arrested or where his family was. When he was shown photos of his dead family members, he cried and claimed he had nothing to do with it. Grant's remaining brother, Jason, was brought into the interrogation room near the end of his questioning. However, Grant still insisted he had nothing to do with the killings. On January 28, Grant Amato was charged with three counts of first-degree murder.

———

In Grant's car, investigators found a note that appeared to have been written by his brother, Cody:

"Grant, I'll take care of all your problems; I just need you back. I can't live without you, brother. I said I'd take care of all your problems at the house and I have. No one will bother you again regarding this. Just please come home."

Although the note appeared to have been written by Cody, Grant later told detectives that he had written it himself. He claimed it was simply a note to himself repeating what his brother had told him. He had no explanation, however, for why it was written from Cody's perspective.

On Grant's computer, investigators found photos of credit cards belonging to Cody, Grant's parents, his aunt Donna, and several other family members.

On July 31, 2019, Grant Amato was found guilty on all three murders and was given a life sentence for each killing.

9

THE PIGGY PALACE

The Downtown Eastside of Vancouver, Canada, has a long history of being one of the worst areas in all of Canada, if not all North America. During the first several decades of the twentieth century, the Downtown Eastside was the bustling retail center of Vancouver. By the 1980s, however, the city center had shifted to the west. This caused the Downtown Eastside to become rundown and overloaded with the homeless, drug addicts, and sex workers. The area became known as "Low Track."

Almost fifty city blocks were inhabited with 7,000 - 10,000 people living in squalor. By the late 1990s, Vancouver had declared the area a public health emergency. Crack cocaine, heroin, and crystal meth were rampant and the rate of HIV infection was rising quickly. Unprotected sex with prostitutes and sharing heroin needles had become the norm. As a result, more than eight percent of the Low Track inhabitants were infected with HIV—the highest infection rate in North America. Throughout the nineties, there was, on average, at least one overdose death on the streets every day.

Prostitution was commonplace in the area. Girls as young as their early teens and women as old as fifty walked the streets looking to turn a quick trick. Some charged as little as $5 for sex, just enough to get their next drug fix. In the mid-nineties it was estimated that there were more than 1,000 sex workers on the Low Track streets. Although only 2% of Canada's inhabitants are Indigenous or Aboriginal Canadians, almost 50% of the sex workers in the area were Indigenous. Most had been sexually abused as children and virtually all of them were addicted to drugs. The Low Track sex workers faced violence on a daily basis—if not from their pimps or johns, then from the police.

But drugs, homelessness, poverty, and prostitution weren't the only problems in the area. Women were disappearing at an alarming rate. As early as 1983, prostitutes in Low Track were mysteriously vanishing. With so many homeless prostitutes on the streets, most of whom used fake names and had no known addresses, authorities didn't notice the trend until almost a decade later. Many sex workers had no known families and no one to report them missing. Those who were formally reported missing were usually reported months or years after they were last seen.

By 1996, dozens of sex workers had been reported missing and more women were added to the list each year. Most cases were noted but not investigated until the summer of 1998, when a group representing indigenous women presented a list to police of women they believed to have been murdered. Police, however, pointed out that many of the alleged victims listed had actually died from HIV or drug overdoses, while others had simply left the Vancouver streets and were reported alive in other cities.

Nonetheless, it prompted detectives to create a more accurate list of missing women from the streets of Low Track. The new list was made up of forty women that had simply vanished without a word and without a body. Some of the missing women were last seen more than a decade prior, but sixteen of those women had been prostitutes in Low Track within the past three years. Police, however, refused to admit that it may have been the work of a serial killer.

Vancouver's Missing Women

In April 1998, police received a missing person's report from a man named Wayne Leng. His twenty-eight-year-old girlfriend, Sarah De Vries, had gone missing while working the streets of Low Track. Just months earlier, she had been picked up by a customer, taken to a rural area, beaten, and left to find her way back to the Low Track. When she reported the incident to police, she was mocked, ridiculed, and sent on her way. When Wayne reported her missing again, police shrugged off the case as another hooker that ran away somewhere. It was a common refrain that many loved ones had received from police when they reported their young female family members missing.

Wayne Leng knew Sarah. He knew she wouldn't just run away from him and their daughter. He put up posters in the area and set up a hotline. Eventually, he received a call from a man named Bill Hiscox, who told him he might want to check a creepy slaughterhouse in Port Coquitlam called The Piggy Palace, run by the Pickton brothers.

———

Police were already familiar with the Pickton brothers. David Pickton had a prior conviction in 1992 for sexual assault. For that offense, he was fined $1,000 and given thirty days' probation. Robert Pickton had been accused of attempted murder in 1997, but served no jail time when the charges were dropped.

Robert and David Pickton grew up working on the pig farm that their parents, Leonard and Louise Pickton, owned seventeen miles east of Vancouver in Port Coquitlam. As children, Robert and his brother helped to raise, feed, and slaughter pigs. Their older sister, Linda, was raised with relatives in Vancouver because their father believed that a pig farm wasn't a place to raise a young girl.

Louise Pickton was the taskmaster of the family and made sure the boys always did their chores. The farm was the number one priority for the family; cleanliness and school were secondary. The boys were regularly sent to school with filthy, unwashed clothes and smelling of pig manure. The other kids nicknamed them "the stinky piggies." Both boys would often skip school just to avoid ridicule from the other children.

At the age of eleven, Robert grew to love a calf that he had purchased with his own money and raised as a pet. One afternoon, when he returned from school, he found his pet calf slaughtered in their barn. A cruel joke that most likely scarred his young mind.

In 1963, Robert dropped out of school at the age of fourteen and took a job as a butcher's apprentice. It was something he had experience with and was good at.

On October 16, 1967, Robert's brother David had just received his driver's license. The two of them went out for a drive when David accidentally hit a young boy walking on a country road. Scared, the boys returned home and told their mother what had happened. Louise was the protector of the family and had a plan. She told the boys to take the truck into the shop to get the dent fixed while she would take care of the boy. Louise Pickton found the boy still alive on the side of the road. But instead of taking him to the hospital, she rolled the boy into a drainage ditch and left him to die. Although it was a suspicious death, no charges were ever made and the death was ruled an accident.

After working for six years as a butcher's apprentice, Robert Pickton returned to the family farm to work full-time. Among his new responsibilities, he purchased pigs at auction, raised and fed them, and then slaughtered them. His new job included disposing of the bits of bone, guts, and parts of the pigs that the family was unable to sell locally. He loaded 55-gallon barrels full of the remains and drove them to an animal waste plant near downtown Vancouver called West Coast Reduction.

It was during these frequent trips to the city that Robert Pickton got his first taste of Low Track. It was at Low Track that he realized he could pay for sex without the worry of anyone noticing that he smelled of sweat and pig manure. No one would call him "stinky piggy" in Low Track. A man with any form of income at all could easily make friends in Low Track—and friends were something that Robert Pickton had never had.

Throughout his twenties, Robert cruised the streets picking up prostitutes. He treated the girls politely, supplied them with drugs, and paid them well. He became known among many of the Low Track prostitutes as a nice, friendly farm boy. It made him feel good that he was able to help people that were obviously down on their luck. But deep inside, Pickton had a rage that would eventually surface.

Just before Robert Pickton's thirtieth birthday, his father died. The following April, his mother died of cancer. Pickton looked after his mother in her dying days and her death hit him hard. He and his two siblings inherited the family farm and all of their parents' belongings, but Robert was the only one of the three that had any interest in the pig farm. Slaughtering pigs was the only craft he knew and he wanted to continue.

Robert moved into a trailer near the slaughterhouse while his brother occupied the main house. For several years, Pickton spent his days working on the farm and cruised Low Track at night, often inviting prostitutes back to the farm. He offered both men and women from Low Track odd jobs on the farm doing what they could—cleaning and helping to feed the pigs. But over time he developed a distaste for the women.

In 1980, not long after his mother's death, Pickton picked up a fourteen-year-old prostitute from the streets of Low Track. According to the girl, they drove to a secluded parking lot and argued over how much she would be paid. Pickton became furious and attacked her. He punched her in the face and raped her at knifepoint before she was able to run from his truck. Afterward, the young girl called Vancouver police —but the police never came. Still needing to pay for a room for the night, she returned to the street to turn another trick.

———

By the mid-1990s, urban sprawl was pushing the suburbs of Vancouver eastward and the land Pickton and his siblings owned became sought after by real estate developers. In 1994, they sold several acres of the land north of the slaughterhouse for more than two million dollars. It was enough money that he and his siblings would never have to work again. But, despite his wealth, Pickton continued to live in the small trailer among the pigs.

In 1996 the Pickton brothers created a non-profit business they called "Piggy Palace Good Times Society." The business claimed to be a charity with the intent to "organize, co-ordinate, manage and operate special events, functions, dances, shows and exhibitions on behalf of service organizations, sports organizations and other worthy groups." In reality, it was just an excuse to have giant rave parties and concerts in the slaughterhouse.

The raves attracted as many as 2,000 people per night and were frequented by many of the prostitutes from Low Track. Not only was Robert Pickton rich, but he was now considered a celebrity among the sex workers. His filthy trailer became his own private sex shack. His sexual needs, however, quickly progressed into more deviant acts. He liked it dirty, like his life on the pig farm.

In March 1997, Pickton had brought a Low Track prostitute named Wendy Eistetter to the farm. Inside his trailer, Pickton handcuffed one of her hands and attempted to cuff the other end to the bed, but she broke free before he locked the other cuff. As she struggled to get away, Pickton stabbed her several times. However, she managed to get the knife away from him in the struggle and stab him as well. This gave Wendy an opportunity to escape. She opened the trailer door and ran as fast as she could from the farm. She quickly flagged down a passerby, who rushed her to a nearby hospital. Pickton was charged with attempted murder, forcible confinement, and assault with a weapon. But, as Eistetter was afraid Pickton would kill her if she testified against him, she dropped the charges.

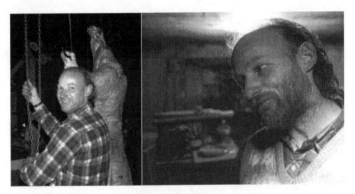

Robert "Willy" Pickton

By the summer of 1997, several dozen women had gone missing from the streets of Low Track. The number was growing every year but Robert Pickton wasn't even on the police's radar—because they weren't looking for anyone. In the eyes of law enforcement, the women were expendable.

They were junkies and hookers that knew what they were getting themselves into. Plus, there was no evidence that they hadn't just hopped on a bus for another city.

That fall, the Pickton brothers were sued by Port Coquitlam for violating zoning ordinances. City officials realized that their non-profit business was just a front to have wild parties in their slaughterhouse. But despite the ordinance against them, the brothers held one last blow-out for a 1998 New Year's Eve party. As a result, an injunction was placed on the organization that removed their non-profit status and gave police the authorization to arrest and remove any person attending any future parties held at the Piggy Palace.

———

Andy Bellwood had worked on the pig farm for only a month. He was one of the many people employed at the farm to clean and do odd jobs. Bellwood had struggled with drug addiction for much of his life and had met a friend while he was in rehab who introduced him to Robert Pickton. Pickton offered Bellwood a job at the farm to help him get his mind off of drugs and get back on his feet.

One night, when Bellwood was alone with Robert Pickton in his trailer, Pickton asked him if he would be interested in hiring a prostitute. Bellwood said no, but Pickton continued, "Do you know what I do with hookers?" Pickton asked. He then pulled three items from beneath his bed: a belt, hand-cuffs, and a roll of metal wire. Pickton then provided a detailed explanation of how he liked to bind, torture, and murder the prostitutes he hired.

Pickton described how he would bring prostitutes to his trailer, handcuff and rape them, and then strangle them with a wire. He claimed that he would then take them out to the barn, hang them, and gut them just like he did to the pigs. What was left of the remains, he ran through a grinder or wood-chipper. "You wouldn't believe how much blood comes out of a human body," he told Bellwood.

Bellwood doubted his nightmarish story. It couldn't possibly be true. He brushed it off as Pickton being weird and creepy and went about his business. Four days later, however, he was accused of stealing farm equipment and beaten up by two men on the farm. The men were sending a message from Pickton. Fearing for his life, Bellwood fled the farm and never returned.

———

For six years, Bill Hiscox had heard stories about the Piggy Palace that kept him awake at night. Horrible stories that he had trouble believing. The stories were so gruesome that he eventually felt compelled to call the Crimestoppers hotline and report what he had heard.

In July 1998, Hiscox told police that his friend, Lisa Yelds, worked on the Pickton pig farm and had seen items in Robert Pickton's possession that she believed belonged to many of the missing women in the news. Hiscox said that some of the items belonged to one of the missing girls, Sarah de Vries, but there were many more. Lisa had told him of purses, bloody clothing, pieces of identification, and other personal items, many of which had been destroyed by Pickton in a burning barrel. Pickton had also mentioned to Lisa that if anyone ever needed to get rid of a body, they should talk to him. He could put a body through his grinder and feed it to the pigs. When questioned by police, however,

Lisa Yelds denied the claim and told police that Hiscox was just another delusional drug addict.

By the end of 1998, nine more women had vanished. There were no bodies—the girls had simply disappeared from the streets. Family members that reported them missing were continually met with indifference by authorities. Marnie Frey's grandmother was one of those family members. Marnie had worked as a prostitute and was addicted to cocaine and heroin. She had been missing without a trace since August 1997, but police discounted her disappearance and refused to investigate.

The number of missing women had grown to fifty by February 1999. In May 1999, hundreds of protesters took to the streets of Vancouver in hopes authorities would step up investigations into the missing women. Twenty-nine-year-old Sereena Abotsway was one of the protesters and was interviewed by reporters about her fear of working the streets. She told reporters that she had a sixth sense that she was safe but, just over a year later, she had disappeared as well.

In the summer of 1999, police received a call from a man named Ron Caldwell. He claimed that a woman he knew, Lynn Ellingsen, who lived on the pig farm, had seen Robert Pickton murder a woman he had picked up. She told him that Pickton had hung a woman named Georgina Papin in the barn by a chain. He had butchered her like he had butchered the pigs. Caldwell, however, was addicted to drug and an unreliable informant. Police said he could barely form coherent sentences. Regardless, detectives brought Lynn Ellingsen in for questioning and she, too, denied the claims, defending Pickton at every turn.

In the fall of 2000, Dinah Taylor, yet another heroin and crack addict, began living on the pig farm after Robert Pickton offered to help get her clean. But in exchange, he tasked her with going to women's shelters to get prostitutes and drug addicts for him. Pickton claimed he wanted to help them but he had other plans. Dinah would frequent the women's shelters and coax the girls back to the pig farm. Not long after Dinah arrived, however, her close friend Andrea Jonesbury was reported missing when she missed a methadone treatment appointment.

———

The potential evidence against Robert Pickton was weak. It was mostly based on speculation and second-hand stories from drug addicts. Despite this, police put him under surveillance in the fall of 1999. Pickton, however, knew he was being watched and the following January, voluntarily showed up at the police station with his girlfriend, Gina Houston. During six hours of interrogation, Pickton was helpful every step of the way. He even invited detectives to come visit the farm. Investigators took him up on his offer and searched the farm and slaughterhouse. However, they found nothing to indicate that anything nefarious had gone on there.

By the end of 2001, the number of missing women had grown to sixty-four. Authorities could no longer deny that there was a problem. An investigative task force was finally created and eighty-five investigators were assigned to the case.

———

On February 2, 2002, police finally received a helpful tip—but it wasn't what they had been expecting. A truck driver who occasionally made deliveries to the farm reported that he had seen illegal firearms in Robert Pickton's trailer. But when investigators arrived, they found much more than firearms. In Pickton's trailer, they found an asthma inhaler that was prescribed to one of the missing women, Sereena Abotsway. It was with that discovery that the task force stopped searching for firearms and began searching for bodies. They obtained new search warrants and finally found a slaughterhouse that had been used to butcher much more than just pigs.

Over the next several months, investigators discovered several IDs belonging to the missing women, bloody women's clothing, and a bucket with Sereena Abotsway's head, hands, and feet hidden in a freezer. Another bucket in the freezer contained the frozen head, hands, and feet of Andrea Joesbury. Both women had gone missing just months earlier.

The walls, floor, and cabinets of a camper that had been parked on the property were covered with blood. A mattress inside the camper was soaked all the way through with blood. A trashcan outside of the camper contained the split-open head of Mona Wilson. Her brain protruded from her skull and was soaking in a deep red sludge.

DNA of missing women was found all over the farm. Teeth and bone fragments were identified as belonging to Georgina Papin, Marnie Frey, Brenda Wolfe, and Mona Wilson. Inside Pickton's trailer, investigators found a .22 handgun with a large dildo attached to the end. A single round of ammunition had been fired through the dildo. They also found a .357 Magnum handgun, handcuffs, night-vision goggles, and a syringe filled with blue liquid. A videotape later surfaced of Pickton telling a friend that a good way to kill a hooker was to inject them with windshield washer liquid.

On February 22, 2002, Robert Pickton was charged with two counts of first-degree murder for the deaths of Serena Abotsway and Mona Wilson. After his arrest, Robert Pickton was placed in a holding cell with an undercover detective. Despite knowing he was being watched by the jail cameras, Pickton admitted to the undercover detective that he had killed forty-nine women. "I was going to do one more, make it an even fifty. That's why I was sloppy. I wanted one more. Make... make the big five-o." He also admitted that he used the waste disposal plant to get rid of the excess body parts.

By April 2002, five more charges were added for the deaths of Jacqueline McDonell, Diane Rock, Andrea Joesbury, Brenda Wolfe, and Heather Bottomley. That September, four more were added: Georgina Papin, Patricia Johnson, Helen Hallmark, and Jennifer Furminger. Four more were added in October and twelve more were added in 2005. In all, Robert Pickton faced twenty-seven charges of first-degree murder, but authorities believed the number of women that Pickton had killed was almost double that.

For almost two years, the entire property of the Pickton pig farm was excavated at a cost of $70 million Canadian dollars. It was the largest forensic investigation in Canada's history. Forensic anthropologists divided the property into grids and used huge fifty-foot conveyor belts and soil sifters to search every piece of earth on the property. However, investigators knew that he may have fed pieces of the women to the pigs, making their search more difficult. In March 2004, Canadian health officials issued a warning that Pickton may have ground up the flesh of the missing women and mixed it with the pork that he had sold to the public.

————

The trial of Robert "Willy" Pickton began in January 2007. With so many cases involved, the judge had divided the cases into two separate trials and one case was dismissed for lack of evidence. The first trial was limited to six murders: Sereena Abotsway, Mona Wilson, Andrea Joesbury, Brenda Wolfe, Marnie Frey, and Georgina Papin. Pickton pleaded not guilty to all charges.

The evidence against him was overwhelming. Many that testified against him were former drug users, prostitutes, or had criminal records. Lynn Ellingsen testified that she had seen Pickton hang Georgina Papin, telling the court, "He walked me to the table and made me look and told me if I was to say anything, I'd be right beside her." His defense team cut down her credibility, however, by pointing out that she was a drug addict and was high the night that she claimed to have seen the killing. The defense claimed that Pickton was a simple farm boy who couldn't have possibly pulled off such an elaborate and extensive killing spree.

The jury deliberated for two weeks before returning with their verdict. Audible gasps and screams were heard in the courtroom as the verdict was read. Robert Pickton was found not guilty on all counts of first-degree murder. The jury didn't believe the murders were premeditated and were unsure if Pickton was the only person involved in the murders. Instead, he was found guilty of second-degree murder in all six cases. He received the maximum sentence for the crimes; twenty-five years in prison with no chance of parole.

In a controversial decision, the twenty remaining murder cases were formally stayed in 2010, meaning that Robert Pickton will not stand trial for the murders of Sarah de Vries, Diane Rock, Cara Ellis, Andrea Borhaven, Kerry Koski, Wendy Crawford, Debra Lynne Jones, Tiffany Drew, Cynthia Feliks, Angela Jardine, Diana Melnick, Jacqueline McDonell, Heather Bottomley, Jennifer Furminger, Helen Hallmark, Patricia Johnson, Heather Chinnock, Tanya Holyk, Sherry Irving, and Inga Hall.

Robert "Willy" Pickton will be eligible for parole on February 22, 2024.

10

WHERE IS HEATHER?

O n a sunny Saturday afternoon in late August 1996, Tim and Karen Walthall had spent the morning planting fall flowers in the front yard of their hillside home. The home sat along the banks of the Ohio River, which acted as the border between Indiana and Kentucky. The Walthall home was on the Indiana side of the river, perched at the top of a sloped grassy driveway just a few hundred yards from the Newburgh Locks and Dam.

As Karen prepared lunch, Tim took a bit of time to relax and peer into the high-powered telescope they had recently purchased. From the eye of the telescope, he could see the barges hauling goods down the river so clearly that he was able to read the serial numbers on the sides of the containers they carried. He could also see the Kentucky side of the Ohio River.

Newburgh, on the Indiana side of the Ohio River, was a growing suburb of Evansville, Indiana, while Henderson County, on the Kentucky side of the river, had endless acres of farmland as far as the eye could see.

Tall trees and a rarely used road on the Kentucky side separated the sandy beaches along the river from the farms in the
distance. Through his telescope, Tim could occasionally see a
deer coming through the trees to drink from the river, but
mostly he just saw young kids who found the beaches a
private place to drink beer and smoke pot.

Saturday, August 26, was different. Instead of wildlife, Tim
saw several boys on all-terrain-vehicles tearing up the sand
on the north end of the shore. "Nuisance," he thought. As he
moved his telescope further south toward the dam that
crossed the river, he saw a young girl placing a folding beach
chair into the edge of the water. She laid her beach towel
over the chair and adjusted the chair flat so she could lie on
her stomach. With a small ice chest by her side, the girl undid
her bikini top at the back so she could get an even tan and
laid with her head facing the river.

Tim Walthall was curious and a little confused. The girl was
in her early twenties, petite, and couldn't have weighed more
than 100 pounds. She really shouldn't be out there alone.
That side of the river wasn't a safe place for a young girl to
be by herself.

Just as Tim called his wife over to the telescope to show her,
he noticed a shirtless man wearing cut-off jean shorts
walking out of the trees behind her. The instant the man
noticed the girl, he paused for several seconds. Then slowly
walked closer. Tim watched, thinking maybe the man in his
late twenties was her boyfriend.

Looking towards the river, the girl didn't notice when the
man took several quick steps—then paused again. From the
way he was stepping, Tim could tell he was trying to sneak
up quietly. The man moved quickly again until he was right
up to the girl and forcefully put his left arm on her back,

placing his full weight on her. With his right hand, he wound her long, wavy, brown hair between his fingers and yanked her up to her feet. Her bathing suit top was out of her reach, so she grabbed the beach towel with one hand and attempted to cover herself. As he jerked her up, Tim could see a silver handgun in the man's hand shining in the sun.

Tim Walthall didn't know what to do. Was he really seeing what he thought he was seeing? He continued watching as the man dragged the girl into the trees and, within a minute, they were gone. The girl's beach chair, bikini top, purse with $7.00 in cash, a notebook, and cooler were left sitting on the banks of the river.

Tim called 911, which put him in touch with the Newburgh, Indiana police. After several minutes of explaining to the dispatch operator what he had seen through his telescope, the operator informed him that he would need to call the Kentucky State Police as the crime had happened on the other side of river and across the state line.

Twenty-five minutes had passed before Tim was able to explain what he had seen to the Kentucky State Police. Although a deputy was able to get to the beach within minutes, the perpetrator and the girl were long gone. Her belongings were still laying by her lone beach chair. The trail of sand leading to the woods provided evidence of a struggle, but no real useable evidence. Police immediately searched the area using police dogs and divers in the river but found nothing.

For the next hour, Tim Walthall explained what he had seen over the phone several times, being passed back and forth to several different officers. Frustrated, he thought it would be easier to just hop in his boat and cross the river to speak directly with the officers on the scene.

Last known location of Heather Teague

Tim claimed, with his high-powered telescope, he could see every part of the abduction as clearly as if he were standing there himself. He saw his black tennis shoes, his jean shorts, he could even see the hairs on his chest. But for some reason, he couldn't seem to explain the face of the abductor in any sort of detail. Something about his face was "fuzzy," Tim told police. "I couldn't tell if he had a full beard or shaggy hair. I think there may have been something over his face."

On the other side of the trees that lined the beach, police found a car that they assumed belonged to the girl. The car was registered to twenty-three-year-old Heather Teague.

———

In the weeks before her disappearance, Heather Teague was troubled. Although she spent her childhood in the tiny town of Clay, Kentucky, fifty miles south of where she was abducted, for the past few months she had been moving from house to house and keeping her belongings in her car.

Heather was barely over five feet tall and weighed only ninety pounds. She was a beautiful young girl with wavy, brown hair that spiraled halfway down her back. In high school, she had been an honor student at the top of her class, homecoming queen, and a cheerleader. She also played basketball and ran track. But after high school, she found herself lost in her own emotions. Her mother, Sarah Teague, said in the weeks before her disappearance that she "wasn't herself." However her boyfriend, Ricky Banken, insisted her disappearance had nothing to do with her personal problems.

———

In the days after Heather's disappearance, a farmer from Kentucky whose property bordered the woods where Heather's car was found came forward with some information. His farmland had been vandalized by kids riding ATVs through his crops and he had hired someone to videotape his fields to catch the vandals. In doing so, the camera had captured Heather's car parked near the edge of the woods. It wasn't the only car, though. Shortly after Heather had parked, another vehicle had parked in the same area: a red and white Ford Bronco. Although Broncos were a common vehicle at the time, this particular Bronco had a distinctive after-market chrome luggage rack attached to the top.

Tim Walthall gave police the best description he could of the man he saw abduct Heather Teague and two composite drawings were released to the local newspapers and television stations. The drawings had triggered several calls to the Kentucky State Police and one name popped up over and over again: Marty Dill. Several callers had reported that a man named Marty Dill resembled the composite sketches that had been released to the media and also drove a red and white Ford Bronco with a chrome luggage rack on top.

As it turned out, Marvin "Marty" Ray Dill was well-known to police on both sides of the river. In 1993, he received a criminal complaint after he made obscene phone calls to a woman whose boyfriend had just been killed. When the woman answered her phone, he asked to speak to her boyfriend. But her boyfriend was dead and Marty Dill knew it. When the woman explained that her boyfriend was dead, Dill laughed and hung up. Later, he followed the woman as she went on dates. After the dates, he called and told her was watching her, saying, "If I wanted to, I could have raped you."

Heather Teague & Marty Dill

A year before Heather went missing, Marty Dill had been a suspect in the rape of a woman in a cemetery near his home-town in Kentucky. Similar to the Heather Teague case, the woman recalled that the man that assaulted her had shoulder-length sandy blonde hair, wore cut-off jeans, and threatened her with a silver handgun. He also wore fishnet over his head to obscure his face. Although he was a suspect in the rape, Dill was never charged and the rapist was never apprehended.

Dill had been arrested on the Indiana side of the river just six months before Heather Teague went missing, when Evansville, Indiana police received a call on February 24 of a man in a red and white Ford Bronco cruising the streets and propositioning young girls for sex.

When police pulled Dill over, they found a loaded .357 Magnum revolver and a .25 caliber semi-automatic pistol. In the back of the Bronco, they found what they believed to be a "murder kit" containing knives, rubber gloves, black plastic trash bags, rope, a shovel, and duct tape. It was clear that his intention had been to kill a young girl that day.

At the time, however, Dill had an outstanding indictment in Kentucky for growing and dealing marijuana and was returned to Kentucky to serve his sentence. He had been sentenced to five years in jail for the marijuana violation but served only forty days before he was released due to overcrowding of the Kentucky prisons. After his release, Kentucky authorities had misplaced his Indiana warrant and Dill was set free rather than returned to Indiana.

─────

In the days after Heather Teague's disappearance, the media reported that the suspect police were looking for drove a red and white Ford Bronco with a chrome luggage rack. Tracy Dill knew right away that her husband was involved.

When Tracy confronted Marty about her suspicions, he blew up at her. "The less you know, the better!" he screamed. He told her that she and their son needed to leave the trailer that they lived in. "Go stay with your brother! The less you know, the better! There's no way I'm going to jail again. If the cops come for me, I'm going to kill myself!"

Tracy Dill knew her husband was involved in the disappearance of the missing girl but she wasn't sure to what extent.
She did as she was told and left Marty Dill in the home.

On Thursday, August 31, police received another anonymous phone call. The male caller claimed to be a friend of
Tracy Dill. The man was calling from a local payphone and
told police that Marty Dill had told his wife to take their son
and leave the property. The man claimed that Marty was
upset when his wife had confronted him about the missing
girl on Newburgh Beach. The caller also let police know that
Marty Dill was contemplating suicide.

That same afternoon, police received another anonymous tip
that Marty Dill was on his property and had hidden his
Bronco deep on his father's twenty-eight-acre property,
which was adjacent to his own property.

By evening, Kentucky State Troopers were stationed all
around the Dill property waiting for a search warrant to be
signed by a judge. By 1:00 A.M. the following morning, the
warrant had been signed and officers approached the trailer.

Marty Dill's father stood outside the blue and white double-
wide trailer and spoke to police as they approached. "Marty
said he's looking at twenty to life if he goes back to jail. He
says he's not going," Dill's father told police.

Just then, a shot rang out from inside the trailer and Marty
Dill's uncle, a retired police officer, ran out. "Marty shot
himself!" he told the police as they ran into the trailer.

Marty was unresponsive on the floor of the trailer, but still
alive. Using a small caliber handgun, he had shot himself in
the right temple. Ambulance crews rushed him to Community Methodist Hospital, where he was pronounced dead just
after 3:00 A.M.

Detectives called Tim Walthall in the middle of the night and asked him to come to the morgue to identify Dill. Without a doubt in Walthall's mind, he told detectives that Marty Dill was the man he had witnessed through his telescope abducting Heather Teague. Detectives also contacted the woman that had been raped in the cemetery and she confirmed that Marty Dill was the man that raped her.

In the weeks after Dill's death, search crews used sniffer dogs to search both Marty Dill and his father's properties. The extensive search, however, turned up nothing. A neighbor, however, came forward and told police that they had heard screams coming from the Dill property just seven hours after Heather had gone missing. The Ford Bronco was found hidden 200 yards into the property but there was no sign of Heather Teague. She had simply vanished. Although the truck had been washed clean, two spots of blood were found inside the Bronco, However, tests showed that one speck was not Heather's. The other was too small to be tested.

While the case was never officially closed, investigators believe that Marty Dill was the man responsible for the abduction of Heather Teague. Although they didn't have a body, they believed she was most likely dead.

———

The confirmation of Marty Dill's death did nothing to stop Sarah Teague's sorrow. Heather's mother was on an endless search for answers. For years, she continued to look.

> "Not a day goes by that I don't think about what happened to
> Heather. I see it in my mind over and over again. I have
> heard she was buried in concrete, fed to hogs, was acciden-
> tally run over trying to escape from a car... everything. The

most horrible thing is that I know that someone knows exactly what happened to her and where she is right now. How can they keep this from a mother? I just don't understand."

Sarah Teague sent Tracy Dill more than twenty letters asking her for any information she may have on her daughter's disappearance. Police believed that Tracy may have helped clean and hide Marty's vehicle but Tracy refused to testify in front of a grand jury, invoking her Fifth Amendment rights. Sarah's attorney questioned if she had destroyed Heather's panties, if Heather had been raped and sold into white slavery, or if she had heard the same screams that the neighbor had heard. Tracy Dill refused to speak. Sarah was eventually charged and arrested for harassing Tracy Dill but was acquitted.

In 2008 Sarah Teague brought bloodhound dogs to the Dill property. Using one of Heather's tennis shoes, the dog handler claimed that after twenty-three years, the dogs were still able to pick up thirteen instances of scents of Heather.

Sarah fought both the Kentucky State Police and the FBI for release of information about the case. She believed that both were withholding information. When the recording of the 911 call from Tim Walthall was released to the public, Sarah and her attorney claimed that it was not the same recording that had originally been played for them. They believed there had been some sort of coverup and the call had been re-recorded later.

Sarah Teague never tired in her search for answers. In 2005, she submitted a sample of her own DNA to the FBI for analysis, who told her that Heather's hair was found on a towel from Marty Dill's Bronco. Sarah, however, had her doubts that Marty Dill was involved at all. According to Dill's family and jail records, his head was shaved at the time of Heather's disappearance. Not shaggy, like Tim Walthall had described. There were also rumors that Dill had only committed suicide because he had been growing marijuana on the property and didn't want to go back to prison for that offense.

Sarah and a private investigator believed it could have been convicted killer Christopher J. Below. Below had been in the area at the time and left Kentucky just after Marty Dill committed suicide. Below had confessed to killing another young woman that resembled Heather Teague but, when asked, denied any involvement in Heather's disappearance.

To this day, Sarah Teague still seeks answers.

11

THE ALLIGATOR MAN

Anyone driving along highway 181, just south of San Antonio, Texas, could easily miss the tiny town of Elmendorf. Today the town is home to less than 1,500 residents, but in the 1930s there were only six hundred people living there.

The Balls had been a prominent family in Elmendorf ever since it was founded in 1885. Frank Ball grew cotton in the area and prospered during the Great Depression by buying real estate when it was dirt cheap. Frank and his wife, Elizabeth, had eight children, most of whom became important figures in the tiny community. One of the children was head of the local school board, another became mayor, another worked as the town's postmaster, and yet another was the head of the church. But none would end up being as well-known as Joe Ball.

Joe Ball was a large man known for his explosive temper and way with women. As a young man he was the first in the area to enlist in the Army during World War I. Just after he returned from the war, the United States entered Prohibition, making it illegal to produce, import, transport, or sell alcohol in any form. Like many others at the time, Joe saw an opportunity and became a bootlegger. Throughout the 1920s, Joe Ball drove around the area of southeast Texas, selling his homemade whiskey out of a fifty-gallon barrel in the back of his truck.

Through the years, Joe became known as a surly drunk that liked to gamble, fight, and take risks. He was large and tough. You didn't want to be on the wrong side of Joe Ball. He was good with a pistol, too—some said he could shoot a silver dollar in mid-air. Throughout the 1920s, he went through two wives and had fleeting relationships with several young women.

When Prohibition ended, the market for his moonshine whiskey dried up. Joe Ball, ever the opportunist, opened a small tavern just off of highway 181 called the "Sociable Inn," but the locals knew it simply as "Joe's Place." The small road-house saloon became a popular hangout for both locals and thirsty travelers. It was known for its rowdy atmosphere, player piano, poker tables, and cheap beer. But the main attractions were the beautiful young waitresses and the five alligators that Joe kept in a cement pond behind the building.

The alligators became a roadside attraction for Joe's Place. As part of the bar's Saturday night entertainment, Joe charged bar patrons to watch him feed them scraps of meat, live cats and dogs, or any sort of wild animal he could get his hands on. Young boys often snuck around the back of the tavern and peered over the fence to watch the carnage.

The Sociable Inn & Joe Ball

Joe treated his employees poorly, particularly if they were black. But one employee, Clifford Wheeler, stuck by his side for years despite being scared to death of him. Joe hired Wheeler, who was in his early twenties, as a handyman to do random tasks around the tavern and any sort of "dirty work" he may need taken care of. Wheeler did whatever Joe Ball told him to do. If he didn't, Joe would shoot at his feet, making him dance until he did as he was told.

Joe Ball wasn't particularly good-looking but he was persuasive. He was able to find scores of young, beautiful women who were eager to work in his tiny saloon. If they didn't mind the rough patrons, they could make more at Joe's Place than in larger cities such as Houston, Dallas, or Corpus Christi. Joe led a strange but comfortable life, but he had one problem—he couldn't seem to keep his waitresses. They just kept disappearing.

Ever since Joe opened the tavern in the early 1930s, his young waitresses would come and go. Some would last a few months while others would be hired on to wait tables, only to disappear without word a week later. It happened so often that many of the regulars at the bar would make jokes that maybe Joe was feeding the girls to the alligators. Little did they know, they may have been onto something.

In the late hours of May 24, 1932, a man surprised Joe Ball as he was carrying what seemed to be a woman's body. Ball was dragging the body from a bedroom in the back of the tavern to the alligator pit behind the building. When Joe saw the man, he pulled his gun on the man and snarled, "beat it!" The man, scared to death, did as he was told but not before Ball threatened him further. He told the man that if he ever told a soul, he would kill him, his wife, and his three children. The man and his family left Elmendorf in fear for their lives.

In 1934, twenty-five-year-old Minnie Gotthardt took a waitressing job at the tavern. "Big Minnie," as she was nicknamed, had a hard edge and no problem handling drunk bar patrons. Joe liked her style and they started a relationship. Minnie and Joe dated for three years but Joe always kept girls on the side.

Joe was also seeing another girl at the tavern named Dolores "Buddy" Goodwin. During a bar fight in the spring of 1937, Joe had thrown a broken bottle at a drunk patron and inadvertently hit Dolores. The bottle gouged her face from her eye to her neck, leaving a permanent scar. Despite the accident, Dolores continued seeing Joe behind Minnie's back. Minnie, however, knew about the affair.

By summer, like so many other female employees at the Sociable Inn, Big Minnie was gone. Joe Ball told his employees and bar patrons that Minnie had left town in a hurry, leaving all of her clothes behind. Again, the jokes started—"Joe fed poor Minnie to the alligators!" He explained, however, that she was embarrassed because she was pregnant with a black man's baby. He claimed Minnie left town to avoid the inevitable small-town gossip.

That September, Joe Ball married Dolores Goodwin. It was his third marriage. As a wedding gift, he told her his dark secret: he had murdered Minnie Gotthardt so they could be together. He confided that he didn't feed her to the alligators, as the men in the bar joked about. He had simply shot her in the head and buried her body in the sand dunes in Ingleside, Texas, near Corpus Christi.

After just four months of marriage, Dolores was in a horrible car accident. She was lucky to be alive but the accident had severed her left arm. Once again, the townsfolk joked that Joe had thrown her into the pit and the alligators ate her arm.

Dolores was good friends with another young girl at the bar, twenty-two-year-old Hazel "Schatzie" Brown. Dolores had a hard time keeping Joe's secret to herself and told Hazel that he had murdered Minnie.

Hazel "Schatzie" Brown & Dolores "Buddy" Goodwin

The news didn't seem to bother Hazel. Despite their close friendship and knowing that Joe was a killer, Hazel and Joe Ball started a relationship. Joe fell in love with the young beautiful brunette and, by April, Dolores, too, had mysteriously disappeared from Elmendorf.

A few months later, Hazel was gone, too.

————

The local Sheriff's department grew understandably suspicious of Ball. The joke of the missing girls had gotten out of hand. It was happening far too often to be a coincidence. Authorities spent the summer of 1938 looking for Ball's wife, Dolores.

On September 23, 1938, a farm hand noticed a horrible stench coming from a greasy fifty-five-gallon barrel behind Joe Ball's sister's barn. The seal on top of the barrel couldn't stop the stench or the flies from swarming around it. It was obvious that something was dead inside. But when Sheriff's deputies arrived the following day, the barrel was gone.

Sheriff's deputies suspected the barrel had contained a body and the jokes flying around town about the missing girls from Joe's Place were starting to seem less like jokes. The first person they wanted to talk to was Joe Ball. At his tavern, Joe told the Sheriff's deputy, who he was friends with, that he didn't know anything about a barrel. Joe's sister, however, confirmed that the barrel had been there the previous day.

That evening, the two Sheriff's deputies went back to Joe's Place and informed him that they would need him to come with them to San Antonio for further questioning. Joe agreed and asked if he could first have a beer and close up the bar for the night. The deputies agreed and followed Joe into the bar, where he cracked himself a beer and took a hard swig. He then rung in a "No Sale" into the cash register to remove the money, but instead reached under the bar and pulled out a .45 caliber pistol. The deputies followed suit and pulled their revolvers. Ball briefly pointed the gun at the deputies then, without blinking an eye, turned the gun on himself and shot a hole in his own chest.

———

With Joe Ball still on the floor behind the bar, investigators searched the area around the alligator pit. On the edges of the pond were bits of rotting flesh and hair, while a nearby axe was covered with blood. Unsure if the blood and hair were human, detectives began questioning employees, starting with Clifford Wheeler.

Clifford Wheeler, a young black man, had been afraid of Joe Ball for most of his adult life. But, now that he was gone, he was quick to talk to police. He explained that the missing barrel behind Joe's sister's barn had contained the body of Hazel Brown, not his wife Dolores Goodwin.

Although she and Joe Ball had been dating at the time, Hazel Brown had met a man at the tavern that she fell in love with. He was a normal man with a normal job that led a normal, respectable life. Like most young girls, she wanted a husband, kids, and a house with a white-picket fence. That wasn't going to happen as long as she worked at a rowdy bar with drunken fights and an alligator pit.

Hazel told Joe Ball she was leaving him and leaving the bar. She said if he didn't let her go, she would tell police that he had killed Minnie. She also suspected that he had killed Dolores. Ball didn't take kindly to the threat and exploded in anger. Clifford Wheeler watched as Joe Ball bludgeoned Hazel to death with the butt of his pistol. At gunpoint, Wheeler helped Ball dismember her body with a saw and the bloody axe that the deputies had found earlier near the alligator pit. Joe Ball and Clifford Wheeler placed her body parts into a fifty-five-gallon barrel and stored it behind Ball's sister's barn.

The body, however, hadn't been fed to the alligators, as the officers had suspected. Wheeler explained that he and Ball later drove the barrel just a few miles out of town and set up camp near the San Antonio River. By campfire light, they dug a grave and emptied the barrel of body parts into the grave. Her clothes and her severed head were burned in the campfire. Wheeler led authorities to the dig site where they unearthed two arms, two legs, and a torso. In the ashes of the campfire they found pieces of her teeth, jawbone, and bits of her skull.

Although Wheeler couldn't explain the disappearance of Ball's wife, Dolores, he knew what happened to Big Minnie. Sixteen months earlier, Ball, Wheeler, and Minnie had driven down to the sand dunes near Ingleside to swim, bask in the sun, and drink beer. Wheeler explained that it was an otherwise normal afternoon picnic until Ball pointed out a bird to Minnie. When she turned her head to look at the bird, Ball shot her in the head. Ball explained to Wheeler that he had gotten her pregnant and he "had to kill her to shut her up." That evening, he and Ball dug a hole in the sand and buried Minnie, who had been pregnant with Ball's child.

Wheeler went on to tell police that Ball was responsible for the murders of several more young women. Possibly as many as twenty, many of which he claimed were fed to the alligators. Although there were plenty of missing women, there was very little evidence to prove more than the two murders.

Three days after Ball shot himself in the chest, Wheeler took detectives to the sand dunes where he and Ball had buried

Minnie Gotthardt. Wheeler drew a large circle in the sand and said, "Miss Minnie is right down here." Dozens of people gathered around the sand to watch while the laborers dug, hoping to catch a glimpse of one of Joe Ball's victims. After nearly a month of digging, they got their wish when the rotting corpse of Big Minnie was pulled from the sand.

Two weeks later, Ball's wife, Dolores Goodwin, was located alive and well in San Diego. She had been arrested for vagrancy after visiting her sister, who lived there. Dolores had nothing but good words to say about her husband:

> "Joe was a bootlegger and a pretty good man. They had him all wrong. He never fed anything live to our alligators, but legend is strong. Why, I lost an arm in an automobile accident and people used to take one look at me and say, 'Joe put her in with the alligators.'"

> "I do know this: Joe never put no people in that alligator tank. I used to get in that tank with the alligators myself and clean it. I'd just push them aside with a broom. They wasn't mean. And anyway, alligators won't eat human flesh. It's sweet and they don't like sweet meat. Everybody knows that."

When asked about Minnie's murder, Dolores said:

> "I was living with Joe then, and I guess you might say he killed her for me. Just before we got married, he told me he'd taken her to Corpus Christi and killed her. He said she wouldn't make us no more trouble. He was drinking and I just couldn't believe him. So I went ahead and married him. Minnie wasn't around anymore."

Regarding the murder of her close friend, Hazel Brown, she told reporters:

> "I didn't see it, but Cliff told me about it. He and Schatzie (Hazel) kept throwing it up to Joe about Minnie. She said he'd killed Minnie and now I was gone, so he must have killed me, too. After a while, Joe hit her with his pistol and I reckon that killed her. Then they cut her up and buried her and tried to burn her head. I sure liked Schatzie."

When police searched Ball's home, they found dozens of love letters and explicit photographs from many of the girls who had gone missing. One letter was from Minnie Gotthardt, where she wrote,

> "I will break you and Dolores Goodman up if it's the last thing I do. I know I may be killed, but who cares?"

After Ball's death, the unidentified man that had moved his family away from Elmendorf returned to tell police his story of witnessing Ball feeding a dead girl's body to the alligators.

For his part in the murders, Clifford Wheeler was sentenced to five years in prison but released after serving two years. After his release, he opened a bar in Elmendorf similar to Joe's Place. But without the alligators.

The five alligators behind the Sociable Inn were donated to the Brackenridge Park Zoo in San Antonio.

12

LIMB FROM LIMB

Thirty-one-year-old Ashley Young was kind and compassionate to a fault. She believed in second chances. Sadly, it was her generosity and forgiveness that would ultimately lead her to the man that would destroy her.

Ashley Young grew up in the small town of Grand Haven, Michigan, along the eastern shores of Lake Michigan. After graduating from Grand Haven High School in 2005, she worked in a local group home assisting mentally-disabled adults. The concept of helping others was ingrained in her by her mother, Kristine Young, who she was very close to. Although Grand Haven was a quaint, idyllic lakeside town, Ashley longed for a larger city where she could attend college.

In 2013, Ashely moved an hour and a half south to Kalamazoo, Michigan, where she enrolled part-time at Kalamazoo Valley Community College. She planned to attend Western Michigan University after graduation.

It was during this time that Ashely met Jared Chance. The two could not have been more different. Ashley was a genuinely caring individual, who felt deep in her bones the need to look out for others. Jared Chance was her polar opposite. He had spent his life looking out for number one—caring only for himself.

———

Despite being raised by a father who had been a deputy police chief, from an early age Jared had a deep hatred of authority resulting in constant conflicts with the law.

Jared Chance grew up in Holland, Michigan, a picturesque city situated along Lake Macatawa that holds its Tulip Time Festival every May to celebrate its Dutch roots. Although Forbes magazine named the city as one of the top five cities in the United States and a Gallup poll named it as the second-happiest and healthiest places to live in America, Jared didn't see it that way.

In his early teens, Jared was caught repeatedly stealing small items and alcohol from local stores. Known as a bully among his schoolmates, Jared constantly fought with classmates, with his parents, and with his younger brother, Konrad. In his teens, he spent time in juvenile detention and had thirty-eight brushes with the law in his first ten years of adulthood.

Many of his arrests were alcohol and marijuana related. One spring at the Tulip Time festival, twenty-year-old Jared was arrested for public intoxication with a blood alcohol level more than double the legal limit. Later that summer, in another drunken incident at his parents' home, Jared head-butted a police officer, breaking the officer's nose. Just nine months later, he was arrested for breaking into the home of his girlfriend by crawling through the dog door.

It was a regular occurrence for Jared's parents, James and Barbara Chance, to call the police on their defiant son. In 2011, his parents called 911 when Jared was drunk and out of control—throwing things around the house and punching holes in the walls. His father told the arresting officer that Jared was not welcome back in their home but, just forty-five minutes later, James forgave his eldest son and Jared came back home. Later that same day, however, police were called a second time. When police arrived, he punched an officer in the head several times before more officers had to use tasers and handcuffs to subdue him.

———

Ashley Young was nurturing and patient with everything she encountered in life. When she met Jared Chance in 2011, she could see that he obviously needed help. Someone to stand by him as a friend and help him bring his life around. Her favorite saying was "If I buy you a smile, would you wear it?" She wanted to buy Jared a smile. Ashley made a point to see the good in people and tried not to judge others.

Ashley Young & Jared Chance / Kristine & Ashley Young

But from the very first days of Jared and Ashley knowing each other in 2011, he fed her an endless stream of lies to gain her sympathy and capitalize on her generosity. Their friendship ended in 2013, when Jared broke into her home, stole her belongings, and sold them.

Ashley was devastated at the abuse of trust but was ever the optimist. Although she broke off ties with Jared, she went on with her life as normal.

―――

Jared moved on as well—in his natural direction, a downward spiral. Jared often fought with his younger brother, Konrad. In 2016, police were called once again to the Chance household. When police arrived to break up the fight, both Jared and Konrad had scrapes and bruises all over their faces. Police asked what the problem was and their father interjected, "Nothing… it was just two brothers arguing." Two days later, however, Konrad contacted the Holland police and relayed the real story.

Konrad admitted to police that Jared had been dealing drugs. He told police that he was trying to steal a five-pound shipment of marijuana that Jared had received from his supplier in California. When Jared caught him, he began beating his younger brother. Jared then lit a blow torch and held it up to his face and threatened to burn him. Jared then let him go, grabbed a stick, and beat Konrad with it, screaming, "I'm going to kill you, you little faggot!"

Just a week later, the two brothers were at it again. Some of Jared's weed had gone missing and he blamed Konrad. When police arrived, Jared claimed that Konrad had thrown hot coffee in his face, while Konrad claimed that Jared had hit him in the head hard enough to give him a concussion. That evening, their father had to separate them. He took Konrad to stay in a hotel room for the night.

Over the next several months of 2016, there were continuous fights between the two boys until one night when Konrad called 911. Jared was unconscious in the backyard of their parents' home—but this time it wasn't from a beating. His mother was administering CPR when the paramedics arrived. He was having an overdose. Four days later, he overdosed again on oxycodone and was given an emergency dose of naloxone, a nasal spray that rapidly reverses an opioid overdose.

The following month, three men with baseball bats beat Jared within inches of his life in the front yard of his own home. Weeks later, Jared called the police, claiming that there were three men wearing camouflage fatigues in his backyard antagonizing him with rifles. When police arrived, however, there were no men there. Jared, most likely high at the time, told police he had taken pictures of them with his phone, but the photos were just a black screen and blurry shots of his feet.

By the end of 2016, Jared Chance had been arrested for possession of methadone and oxycodone. He was placed on probation but violated it multiple times. He had three felony offenses under his belt. A fourth offense would make him a habitual offender and could mean a life sentence.

———

In 2017, Jared moved forty miles east from the family home in Holland, to Grand Rapids, Michigan. Ashley was living an hour south in Kalamazoo and working at a call center for PNC Bank while she went to school.

It had been four years since Jared had abused her trust and stolen things from her apartment. At the encouragement of a mutual friend, Ashley reached out to Jared through Facebook. She told him that she had forgiven him for what he had done and was willing to be friends again. Jared, of course, jumped at the chance.

In late 2018, life on her own was finally starting to take shape for Ashley. She had just found an apartment she wanted to rent but needed a co-signer. Her mother, Kristine Young, was more than happy to help.

Kristine and Ashley were scheduled to meet on November 29, 2018, to sign the lease to the new apartment, but Ashley told her mother that she was driving up to Grand Rapids the night before to visit with a friend. She didn't want to tell her mother that she was meeting with Jared Chance. Ashley knew she wouldn't approve. She had told her mother that she'd been speaking to Jared again, but Kristine had no idea that Ashley had plans to meet with him. Kristine knew there was nothing good that could come from visiting Jared Chance. He was trouble.

Kristine also hadn't known that Ashley had already met with Jared earlier that year. Jared had been driving drunk through Kalamazoo and crashed his car into a ditch. The first person he called for help was Ashley. Ashley, eager to help, drove Jared back home to Grand Rapids.

———

On Wednesday afternoon, Ashley Young drove the one-hour trip up to Jared's apartment in Grand Rapids. Jared lived in the upstairs unit of a duplex home at 922 Franklin Street. When she arrived, the two visited with Jared's downstairs neighbor, Mario Nelson, for a while before they drove to Mulligan's Pub about a mile away.

Emily Potgetter, a bartender at Mulligan's Pub, noticed nothing out of the ordinary as she served them shots of tequila and beer. Jared and Ashley walked back and forth a few times between Mulligan's and a hookah lounge across the street that night before they left just after 1:30 A.M. A security camera at a nearby business caught the last glimpse of Ashley alive.

———

Kristine Young knew something was wrong when Ashley hadn't shown up to sign the lease papers for her new apartment that morning. It wasn't like her. Ashley was ecstatic to move in and wouldn't have missed it for the world. When she received no answer to calls and texts sent to Ashley's phone, Kristine began to panic.

Kristine knew that Ashley had gone to Grand Rapids to visit a friend but didn't know who. She frantically left voicemails on her phone but received no reply. That's when she got on Facebook and began messaging Ashley's friends to see if they knew who she was with the night before. Her heart sank when she learned that Ashley had gone for drinks with Jared Chance. After several more messages to Ashley's friends, Kristine was able to get Jared's phone number.

Kristine sent several texts and calls to Jared's cell phone, which went ignored. She finally left a stern voicemail:

"Hello Jared, my name is Kristine Young. I am looking for my daughter. She was last with you. Is she with you? She needs to contact me. Tell her I am going to contact the police department to do a missing person."

Jared finally replied via several casually worded text messages. He claimed that Ashley had lost her cell phone at Mulligan's Pub the night before. She had gone back to collect it and then would drive back to Kalamazoo. He gave Kristine several random phone numbers to call in order to locate her daughter, but each number he gave was a dead end. Wrong numbers and disconnected numbers. He was making it up as he went along. Kristine knew he was lying and something horrible had happened.

Over and over, Jared made excuses. He told Kristine that he thought she was with her ex-boyfriend and maybe she wasn't calling her back because she knew that Kristine was mad at her.

Jared fed her lie after lie. He eventually said he had spoken to Ashely just minutes ago -- she was at a friend's house. He gave Kristine the phone number of his friend, Demetreis Taylor, saying that he had just spoken to Ashley there and if she called quick, she could talk to her. He quickly messaged Demetreis, who lived in Kalamazoo, and told him that he would be getting a call from Kristine Taylor. Jared told him to lie to Ashley's mother and tell her that Ashley was at his house, used his phone, then left for Kalamazoo.

Demetreis was having none of it. He knew Jared well enough to know that he didn't want to be involved. When Kristine called, Demetreis told the truth and said Jared had lied to her. Demetreis had never even met her daughter. Jared then tried to cover his tracks and told Demetreis to delete any record of their conversation.

All day on November 30 and into December 1, Jared strung Ashley's mother along with lie after lie.

On December 1, Kristine drove to the Grand Rapids Police Department to report Ashley missing. The police, however, told her it wasn't possible to file a missing person report yet. Ashley was an adult and had only been missing for three days. Frustrated, Kristine and Ashley's friends got the word out about her disappearance using social media and directly implicated Jared Chance in the posts.

———

In the afternoon of December 1, Jared's father James, his mother Barbara, and his brother Konrad drove their Honda CRV from Holland to Grand Rapids to pick up Jared and bring him home for the night. Jared was clearly upset.

Jared asked his brother to help him load two large, heavy boxes into the back of the SUV. One box contained sealed black plastic garbage bags. He also put a mop and bucket, Skilsaw, and a shower curtain in the back of the car. Before they left Grand Rapids, Jared asked his father to stop at

Ashley's car, which had been parked about a mile from his house. Jared opened the car and collected a black pair of boots and a few other things from inside. The family then continued heading toward Holland, stopping briefly at Costco on the way home.

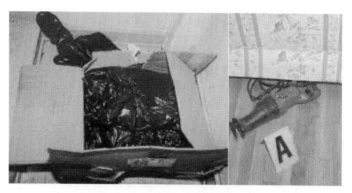

Box containing Ashley Young's limbs / Skilsaw

That evening, Jared made a fire in the back yard of the family home, doing his best to throw in some of the items from the boxes that he had brought from Grand Rapids. Konrad could tell something was troubling his older brother and, after some prodding, Jared admitted that he had murdered Ashley Young.

The two boys then shared the news with their parents. Jared's father, James Chance, was a retired police officer. This put him in a unique position to know what to do in situations like this.

On the morning of December 2, Jared and his father traveled back to the Grand Rapids Police Department. Together, they walked to the window and told the desk clerk that they had information about a missing person's case.

James told the officers that his son was being harassed on Facebook by the missing girl's friends and family and was willing to come in to answer questions. But when the officers asked when he last saw Ashley Young, James immediately interjected and said, "My son isn't talking to anyone without an attorney."

The officer told James and Jared that an attorney isn't just provided for someone that walks in the door and says, "You have to provide me an attorney." At that point, he wasn't under arrest and the police had no authority to detain him—and James Chance knew that. He told the officers, "This is your last chance. You're gonna let him leave? You're making the biggest mistake of your career." Jared and James Chance then walked out the door.

Jared and his father drove back to Holland and packed the boxes, mop and bucket, and several other items back into the Honda CRV. Late that morning, Konrad drove Jared back to his apartment in Grand Rapids and dropped him off.

———

In the early evening of December 2nd, Jared's downstairs neighbor, Mario Nelson, and his girlfriend noticed a horrible smell. But they weren't quite sure where it was coming from. They walked outside and followed the stench to the back of the house. Once Mario poked his head in the basement door, he knew it was the source. Mario crept down the stairs and noticed a tarp covering something on the landing of the stairs. When the light hit the tarp, he saw that a dark liquid had seeped out from under the tarp and knew it was something bad. He called police immediately.

When officers arrived and looked beneath the black tarp, they found a female torso in a dark pool of blood. The head, legs, and arms had been removed. Further searches of the basement produced a saw blade and 429 unspent .22 caliber cartridges. Hidden in the building's furnace duct were two spent .22 caliber shell casings.

When officers asked Mario Nelson if he knew of anyone in the building that owned a .22 caliber gun, he pointed upstairs and said, "Jared Chance." Mario told the police that, a few days earlier, he had briefly met Ashley Young. The day Ashley went missing, Jared had asked Mario for help getting into her car, which had been parked in their driveway.

Mario later told detectives that Jared had recently shown him a .22 caliber gun. He had spun the gun around on the kitchen table, making Mario nervous. Jared then bragged that if the need ever arose, he knew how to get rid of a body, blood, and fingerprints because his father, a retired deputy police chief, used to be in the Irish mob.

———

Jared Chance was arrested at his apartment late that evening. Outside the door of his upstairs apartment was a pair of black women's boots, a purple tote bag, and the two boxes that had traveled to and from his parents' home. The largest box still had a shipping label on it addressed to Jared Chance. Inside the box was a black plastic garbage bag containing the arms and legs of Ashley Young, minus her hands and feet. The smaller box contained duct tape, black plastic garbage bags, blood-stained bedding, and women's clothing. The purple tote bag held a pair of shoes, plastic shower curtain rings, and a prescription medication bottle with Ashley Young's name on it.

Inside Jared's apartment, investigators found traces of blood on the stairwell, in his bathtub, and in the kitchen, the latter of which was accompanied by pieces of human tissue. Pants with his name on them, a black hoodie, and a bathmat all tested positive for blood, as did the inside of the washing machine. The kitchen drain trap held small pieces of human tissue and a utility knife had lodged in the toilet drain trap.

Outside of the home, police found the mop that he had initially taken to his parents' house. The mop was placed next to a black trashcan that contained another pair of Jared Chance's jeans, two additional saw blades, a bathtub drain cover, more black trash bags, a roll of plastic wrap, latex gloves, and an empty bottle of ammonia. Additional shower curtain rings were found in the backyard.

———

Jared was charged with the mutilation of a dead body and concealing a death. Initially, he wasn't charged with murder since the head, hands, and feet were not found. Although it was believed that it was the body of Ashley Young, it couldn't immediately be identified.

Jared was calm and showed very little emotion when arrested. During questioning, he again asked to speak to an attorney before answering any questions.

Two days later, a search warrant was issued for the home of James and Barbara Chance in Holland. There they found the shower curtain that was missing from Jared's apartment, while hidden beneath a couch in the living room was a red and black electric Skilsaw with bits of human flesh on it. A bloody washcloth was found in the basement. Their Honda CRV had human bloodstains on the rear carpet, where the boxes sat. An empty box of latex gloves and an empty bottle of ammonia still lay in the back of the SUV. The price sticker on the ammonia bottle read "Miss Tracy's Party Store"— located just around the corner from Jared's home.

Investigators checked security cameras from Miss Tracy's Party Store between the days of November 29 and December 1. Jared was seen in the store on several occasions buying ammonia, black plastic garbage bags, and other items. The cameras also showed him placing something in the trashcan outside of the store.

When detectives searched trashcans and dumpsters near Miss Tracy's Party Store, they recovered an orange plastic bag containing more clothing that tested positive for human blood, Ashley's purse with her driver's license, and prescription medication bottles with Ashley's name on them.

———

On December 7, DNA results showed positively that the recovered body parts were indeed those of Ashley Young. Jared Chance was charged with open murder and four counts of tampering with evidence on January 3, 2018. A forensic pathologist was unable to determine an actual cause of death since the head, hands, and feet were never recovered. However, by process of elimination, the pathologist believed that the cause of death was the result of trauma to the head or neck. It was determined that she most likely died due to a gunshot wound or blunt force trauma, but there was no way to be certain without the head.

Days later, Jared's parents, seventy-six-year-old James Chance and sixty-three-year-old Barbara Chance, were arrested and charged with perjury and being accessories after the fact. On December 12, they each posted $25,000 bail and surrendered their passports. They adamantly denied any guilt, despite having transported body parts for their son and helped him escape detection. The accessory after the fact charge was a felony which carried a possible five-year sentence. The perjury charge was a potential life sentence.

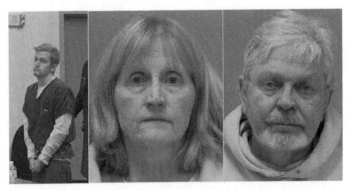

Jared, Barbara, and James Chance

Prosecutors spent the next twenty months developing a case against Jared Chance and his parents. Evidence was gathered from surveillance cameras from businesses near Mulligan's Pub and the Hookah lounge. Prosecutors also learned that the family hadn't disclosed that they had stopped at Costco with Ashley's arms and legs in the back of their Honda. That stop would have given Jared an opportunity to get rid of a murder weapon and body parts.

———

Kristine Young and Ashley's extended friends and family wanted closure, but Jared Chance was saying nothing. Ashley's remains would never be whole without her head, hands, and feet. In September 2019, Jared Chance was offered a deal. If he provided the location of Ashley's remains and pleaded guilty to a lesser charge of second-degree murder, tampering with evidence, mutilation of a dead body, and concealing a death, he could avoid a trial and receive a lighter sentence. Because this was his fourth offense as a habitual offender, he would be sentenced to a minimum of thirty-one years in prison. However, it also meant that there was a chance that, someday, he may see the light of day outside of a prison. The other option was to face a jury and risk a guilty verdict and a likely lifetime behind bars.

Up until days before the trial, most people involved expected the trial to not happen. Everyone assumed he would take the deal. Jared Chance had already lied repeatedly to Ashley's mother by concealing her death but, ultimately, he refused to give her the slightest bit of closure and turned down the deal.

———

During the trial of Jared Chance in September 2019, Kalamazoo officers explained what they had found at his apartment during the investigation. Jurors were shown crime scene photos, including the dismembered arms and legs. Mario Nelson gave his account of when he first found the tarp-covered torso by following the horrible stench. Ashley's mother, Kristine, read aloud Jared's deceptive text messages one-by-one as jurors read them on a large display screen. Jared's brother Konrad testified of the events of the day he and his parents helped Jared move boxes containing Ashley's remains and when he admitted that he had killed Ashley. After less than a week of testimony of those involved and from forensic experts, the jury unanimously pronounced Jared Chance guilty on all accounts.

Jared Chance / Konrad Chance / Demetreis Taylor / Mario Nelson

On October 10, 2019, Jared Chance was sentenced from a minimum of 100 years in prison to a maximum of 200 years. Judge Mark Trusock's sentence was far and above the recommended sentencing guidelines of twenty-two and a half to seventy-five years. However, the judge declared that he wanted to make sure that Chance would never be released.

> "What you did was reprehensible and heinous. You, sir, in my mind, are a very evil individual. You are clearly a monster without any conscience. You are someone who is a danger to society and should never be allowed free. I am purposely doing this so that you will not be eligible for parole until you are 130 years old. The guidelines do not take into account the level of brutality involved and your lack of compassion and remorse."

Kristine Young faced Jared Chance at the sentencing hearing holding a box that held Ashley's ashes. She screamed nearly every word of her victim impact statement directly facing him, bringing the courtroom to tears.

"Jared Chance, I hate you! I want to rip you limb from limb and discard you, just like you did to Ashley! I cry seven days a week! You threw her out like trash and she was your friend! Why? …If I want a hug, I have to hug a box!"

In January 2020, Barbara Chance pleaded no contest to the charges of perjury and being an accessory after the fact. James Chance took his case to trial. During the trial, the prosecution attempted to prove that James intentionally omitted details about where they had stopped when they carried Ashley's body parts in the back of his Honda. They said the omission affected the gathering of evidence, recovery of Ashley's remains, and gave Jared the opportunity to dispose of evidence. James, however, claimed that he only omitted that they had stopped at Costco because of a memory lapse due to old age. Chance claimed that he had a bad memory and often mixed up dates and names, even the names of his two sons. Prosecutors believed that James Chance used his specialized skill from years in law enforcement to help his son get away with murder.

Konrad Chance testified at his father's trial, again telling the story of the day they loaded the family SUV with Ashley's mutilated remains and drove to Holland.

During James Chance's testimony, he said of Jared, "He was crying. He was emotional. He said 'I can't believe I did it, but I was so afraid' and he got this felony thing over his head and he was so afraid and he was extremely under the influence and that's when he proceeded to hack this poor girl up. He indicated to me that he went all over town and put parts in trash bins. I figured the pieces were not in the box because I didn't smell anything. I didn't go digging around in it."

James Chance was found guilty. But despite carrying a mutilated body in his car and a bloody Skilsaw being found beneath his couch, he was sentenced to only thirty days in jail. Barbara Chance was sentenced to only forty-five days. Each also received a year of probation. Kristine Young and friends of Ashley believed that James Chance was given special treatment because of his career in law enforcement.

13

BONUS CHAPTER: THE HOMESCHOOLERS

This chapter is a **free bonus chapter** from True Crime Case Histories: Volume 5

———

It's not clear what life was like for Hana Alemu in Ethiopia, but it's hard to imagine it could have been worse than it became when the eleven-year-old was adopted by the Williams family in Sedro-Woolley, Washington.

———

Larry and Carri already had seven children of their own and wanted more, but her last pregnancy had left Carri Williams unable to bear more children. It had become a trend for homeschooling evangelical Christians in the mid-2000s to adopt needy children into their already large families. The families felt that it was a duty of their faith to rescue children that needed a good home and then homeschool them according to a conservative Christian curriculum. Other

families from their Bible study group had adopted as many
as eight children into their lives; Carri and Larry wanted the
same.

Larry Williams worked from noon until midnight as a mill-
wright for Boeing, while Carri stayed home to homeschool
their kids. Carri had attended a women's retreat run by a
ministry called Above Rubies. During the retreat, they spoke
of the trend among evangelicals to adopt children from
Liberia, a west African country experiencing political insta-
bility caused by multiple civil wars.

In 2008, the Williamses contacted Adoption Advocates
International (AAI), a secular adoption agency based in Port
Angeles, Washington. AAI was run by a woman named
Merrily Ripley who had twenty children; three biological
and seventeen adopted. Merrily informed Carri that there
were two orphaned children in Ethiopia that needed a loving
home. One child was deaf and Carri had studied American
Sign Language before getting married, so it seemed like a
perfect match.

To prepare for the adoption, the Williamses took a quick
home-study course provided by AAI and filled out the necessary paperwork. AAI apparently missed the fact that Carri
had left one section of the paperwork blank: the part about
their beliefs on child discipline.

———

In the months leading up to the adoption, Carri and Larry
saw a one-minute video clip of the children crying and
begging for a good home. It was heart wrenching. Seven-
year-old Immanuel was deaf and eleven-year-old Hana was
slightly underweight at only 77 pounds.

Immanuel and Hana had been living in the Kidane Mehret orphanage in the Ethiopian capital city of Addis Abada. Both had been abandoned at an early age. Though they were not related, they were excited that they would soon become brother and sister living in the United States. Learning that their new parents lived in the idyllic countryside of the Pacific Northwest, Hana naively read *Little House on the Prairie* in preparation for her new, exciting life.

Hana Williams (Right photo in Ethiopia)

In the months after Hana and Immanuel's arrival in 2008, the Williams' post-adoption reports came to AAI as per the adoption agreement. According to the adoption agency, everything in the reports seemed normal and Hana had filled out to a healthier 105 pounds. However, in June 2009, the reports suddenly stopped. Although the adoption agreement stated that Carri and Larry would continue to send reports throughout the children's lives, technically they were under no legal obligation to file the reports. The adoption agency had no way of knowing the atrocities that were going on in the Williams household.

Larry and Carri Williams believed in a strict fundamentalist Christian lifestyle. In addition to homeschooling their children, almost all television and Internet access was prohibited. They believed women should never wear pants, only skirts or dresses and never swimsuits, and certainly never vote. The children were rarely seen in a public setting and only socialized with a select few like-minded families. Larry regularly preached to the children in the backyard of their rural five-acre property.

As for disciplining the children, the Williamses adhered to the teachings of a controversial book called *To Train Up A Child* by Michael and Debi Pearl. The book taught that the principles and techniques for training an animal and raising a child were the same. It instructed parents to begin spanking their children within the first few months of birth to "break their will."

In his book, Michael Pearl's argument for beating a child came straight from his interpretation of the Bible. Pearl believed that Proverbs 13:24 justified his beliefs:

"He that spareth his rod hateth his son."

Pearl said,

"A child properly and timely spanked is healed in the soul and restored to wholeness of spirit. A child can be turned back from the road to hell through proper spankings."

The book went into great detail of specific implements for parents to use; a wooden spoon, spatula, or the most popular weapon — a short length of small plastic plumbing tubing. This was a particularly well-liked implement because it could be easily curled up and kept available in a parent's pocket at all times. The book also taught parents to withhold food and put children under a cold outdoor garden hose as punishment.

The Pearls' book was extremely popular with fundamentalist Christian homeschoolers and, according to the author, sold almost 700,000 copies in the first seven years of its publication. The Pearls' No Greater Joy ministry generated upwards of $1.7 million tax-free dollars per year.

———

For the next two years, Hana's hopes of the American dream quickly washed away. Life with the Williams family was nothing like the *Little House on the Prairie* life she had envisioned.

Within months after Hana arrived in the United States, she began menstruating. This infuriated Carri, who told members of her knitting group that she had wanted to adopt "a little girl, not a half-grown woman." She complained that Hana was rebellious, telling her knitting friends, "I wouldn't wish her on anyone."

Friends and neighbors of the Williams family had noticed that Hana and Immanuel were often absent from public family outings, holidays, trips to town, or to church. On the rare occasion that they were brought to church with the family, one parishioner that knew sign language often attempted to sign with Immanuel, but Carri and Larry didn't want him communicating with anyone. One of them would quickly whisk the boy away before he had a chance to converse.

Neighbors noticed the seven children would be seen actively playing together at the front of the Williams' home, while

Hana and Immanuel would be left standing alone near the driveway staring at their feet.

At home, the discipline was much worse than anyone could have imagined. Hana had Hepatitis B, which again infuriated Carri, who accused her of purposely smearing blood on the bathroom walls. Because of this, Hana was not allowed to use the bathroom in the house. She was only allowed to use a filthy outdoor portable toilet behind the barn that was only serviced twice a year.

The indoor shower was off limits too. Regardless of temperature, Hana's shower was a garden hose propped up with sticks in the front yard. Hana was often forced to use the cold makeshift shower while the other children watched from the windows of the warm house.

When Hana made any sort of complaint about the clothes that Carri had chosen for her to wear, she would lose her right to wear clothes at all, and given only a towel to wear for the day.

Hana had long braided hair that she was proud of. Her hair was the one thing she could take pride in and Carri knew it. The first spring of Hana's new life, she was told to cut the grass in the yard. When she finished, the grass was cut shorter than Carri had wanted it. As punishment, Carri shaved her head. She would later shave her head on two additional occasions.

The daily punishments had begun almost immediately after the children were adopted. Most of the time, Immanuel and Hana had no idea why they were being punished. It could have been for standing in the wrong place or getting an answer wrong on their schoolwork. They were never quite sure.

A few months after arriving in the United States, traumatized by the change of environment and daily punishments, Immanuel began wetting the bed. Carri and Larry were convinced he was doing it on purpose just to anger them. The boy was taken outside and was given a shower with the cold hose, then sent to sleep in the dark shower room.

To add to his trauma, Carri often teased him by running the plastic tubing she called her "switch" up and down his face. On one occasion, Larry hit Immanuel on the top of the head with his fist and caused blood to run down his face. That night, he was made to sleep outside and the other children were told not to sign with him.

The punishments themselves were often straight from the *To Train Up A Child* book and involved beatings with a piece of plastic tubing that Carri kept in her bra. Sometimes it was one of Larry's belts folded in half, or a long, flexible piece of glue stick. Other common forms of punishment that the Williamses adhered to from the book included denying food, denying clothes, forced outdoor sleeping, and cold outdoor showers.

The Williams' biological children were punished, too, but never to the severity of Hana and Immanuel. The adopted children were fed different meals than the biological children. While the other children had sandwiches, Hana and Immanuel would have the same sandwich, but with a glass of water poured over it. Sometimes they would get cold leftovers with unheated frozen vegetables. Almost always, the two children were forced to eat outside while the other children ate inside, regardless of the cold, rain, or snow.

Because of Hana's menstruation, Larry and Carri took the initial steps to change her official age. Carri told her knitting group that if they could get her age bumped up a few years, they could kick her out of the house sooner when she turned eighteen. When another member of the knitting group asked how the girl would survive in the outside world, Carri snipped, "It wouldn't be my problem."

In the three years that Hana lived with the Williamses, she went from sleeping alone in the barn behind the house, to being locked inside a bathroom with no light, to eventually being kept in a four-foot by two-foot closet for up to twenty-four hours at a time. Larry's recorded bible sermons and religious music played outside of the closet the entire time, depriving her of sleep.

———

In the afternoon of Wednesday, May 11, 2011, Carri sent Hana into the backyard as one of her daily punishments. It was a rainy spring day and the temperature was in the mid-forties. When Hana, only wearing shorts and a t-shirt, complained that she was cold, Carri commanded that she do jumping jacks in the yard to stay warm. After a few hours alone outside, the children noticed Hana's lower lip quivering. She seemed unable to control her own movements, had fallen a few times, and eventually had trouble standing up at all.

Carrie went out the back door of the home and grabbed Hana by the arm and led her to the outhouse behind the barn. She continued to fall repeatedly, which infuriated Carri. She believed Hana was only trying to create attention. Unable to get her to stand, Carri left her lying alone in the yard.

Hours later, Hana's clothes were soaked. Carri set dry clothes on the back porch and yelled at her to come back inside the house. When Hana didn't return, Carri called on her two eldest sons. She gave the boys a length of plastic tubing and told them to hit her on her bottom for not following orders. Strangely, as the boys whipped her, she started to remove her own clothing and Carri called the boys back inside. By 5:00 P.M. Hana began throwing herself down on the pavement, gravel driveway, and grass. Her knees and hands began to bloody as Carri watched from inside the warm house. When she couldn't watch anymore, Carri turned away from the window and ignored Hana for the rest of the evening.

Near midnight, the seven biological Williams children giggled as they continued to stare out the window at Hana, who had removed all of her clothing and was still uncontrollably throwing her body around in a fit. She was wallowing in the mud and pounding her own head into the ground. They watched in amusement as Hana was experiencing what's known as "paradoxical undressing." In the final stages of hypothermia, the nerves can become damaged causing irrational behavior. This final stage of hypothermia tricks the mind into thinking it's extremely hot, causing the person to remove their clothes and attempt to burrow themselves into the ground.

When Hana finally stopped moving, one of the daughters called their mother to come check on Hana. She was face-down in the yard with a mouth full of mud. Carri, upset with Hana's nudity, grabbed a bedsheet and wrapped it around Hana. She then instructed her boys to drag her into the house.

First Carri called Larry, who was driving home from work. When she hung up, she finally dialed 911.

"I think my daughter just killed herself.... She's really rebellious, and she's been outside, refusing to come in. And she's
been throwing herself all around. And then she collapsed."

"Is she breathing?"

"I don't think so, no."

"How old is your daughter?"

"I don't know. We adopted her almost three years ago."

"You don't know how old she is?"

"She's somewhere between the ages of fourteen and sixteen.
She was throwing herself all over the gravel, the yard, the
patio. We went to bring her in. My sons tried to carry her in,
and she took her clothes off. She's very passive-aggressive. I
don't know how to describe it."

During the call, Carri sounded more annoyed than saddened
or shocked. The 911 operator coached Carri through CPR,
but it was no use. Hana was gone. When emergency crews
arrived, Hana had a large lump on her forehead and she was
covered in blood. Her hips, knees, elbows, and face had fresh
red bloody markings from repeated whippings. She also had
a stomach infection.

The postmortem examination of Hana's body revealed she
was abnormally thin for just thirteen years old. At only five
feet tall, she was emaciated and had gone back down to 76
pounds. She was lighter than 97% of girls her age and thinner
than she was when she originally came from Ethiopia three
years earlier. The official cause of death was hypothermia
compounded by malnutrition and gastritis (stomach infection). It was determined that her body had been too thin to
retain enough heat on the day she died.

When Child Protective Services knocked on the door of the Williams home the following day, Larry refused to let them in. Two weeks after Hana's death, the entire family were interviewed by detectives and Child Protective Services. All the children gave the same story, obviously coached by their parents: Hana was rebellious and "possessed by demons."

When Immanuel was interviewed, he told detectives, "People like Hana got spankings for lying and go into the fires of Hell." When Larry heard Immanuel give that answer, he immediately stopped the interview and took the children home.

Two months had gone by with no charges brought against the Williamses when Child Protective Services received an anonymous tip. Someone claimed that Carri didn't like her adopted children and Immanuel was being treated much like Hana. With that news, CPS worked with detectives and opened a formal investigation. All eight of the Williams children were taken into foster care. During a search of the house, police found a copy of the book *To Train Up a Child*.

Even after months in foster care, Immanuel was afraid of his foster parents and nervously apologized for every little mistake he made, even asking his foster mother why she wasn't beating him. He told his therapists of repeated nightmares and constantly worried that he would be the next to die. Immanuel was diagnosed with post-traumatic stress disorder.

That September, more than four months after Hana's death, Carri and Larry Williams were arrested on charges of homicide by abuse and first-degree manslaughter for the death of

Hana, as well as first-degree assault of a child for the abuse of Immanuel.

Carri and Larry each faced a potential life sentence. Both posted bail of $150,000 each, but were given strict orders to not contact each other or any of their children — either directly or through third parties or other means. However, when Larry continued to send highlighted bible verses to the children, the prosecution believed them to be coded messages encouraging them to come to his defense. Larry Williams was arrested again and placed in a state jail where he remained for almost two years awaiting trial.

————

This wasn't the first time that the book by Michael and Debi Pearl, *To Train Up a Child,* had been linked to a child's death. Two other sets of fundamental Christian parents that employed tactics from the book had recently killed their adopted children: Sean Paddock and Lydia Schatz. The three deaths happened in different parts of the United States, but all were adopted, homeschooled, and beaten with a length of 1/4 inch plastic tubing, as recommended by Michael Pearl.

Seven-year-old Lydia Schatz's parents, Kevin and Elizabeth, held her down and beat her for nine hours with a piece of the tubing for pronouncing the word "pulled" incorrectly. Four-year-old Sean Paddock's mother Lynn Paddock smothered him in a blanket wrapped too tightly around him because she wanted to stop him from getting out of bed in the middle of the night. Like Hana, the abuse that eventually killed these children was just the tip of the iceberg.

————

At trial, Carri and Larry turned on each other. The couple sat at opposite tables in the courtroom, rarely looking each other in the eye. Larry testified that the discipline was all at the hands of Carri, while Carri testified that her discipline was at the instruction of her husband. Carri also admitted that she told her children not to talk to detectives about any of the abuse. The children, however, testified that lying was considered one of the most serious offenses in their household.

One of the Williams children, Joshua, confirmed that Hana had not been homeschooled or eaten meals with the other children for at least a year before her death. The child told the court that she would sometimes go two days without anyone speaking to her and none of the biological children liked her, "but it didn't matter because she was always in the closet."

Larry, Carri, & Joshua Williams

Immanuel testified using sign language with the help of three interpreters. The courtroom was silent as he was asked what he thought happened to Hana. "I don't know" he signed. "She disappeared. I think maybe she's dead." He also testified that he was often beaten with a stick or plastic tubing until blood ran down his face, telling the court, "I would suffer with the pain until it eventually went away."

The biological children admitted that they were coached to tell authorities that Hana slept in the bedroom with them, when in fact she slept in a tiny locked closet. The jury was shown the closet that she slept in and were shown photos of the scars on Hana's body from repeated beatings.

Larry testified that he trusted his wife's discipline choices with the adopted children because she had done such a good job raising the other children. Carri rebutted that her husband was an equal participant in the discipline and even came up with some methods on his own, like hosing off Immanuel and locking him in the shower room after his bedwetting. She also testified that Larry was the one that installed the lock on the closet door.

During the trial, the defense attempted to argue that Hana was actually sixteen-years old rather than thirteen. If she had been sixteen at the time of her death, the homicide-by-abuse charge could not be applied as it only applies to children younger than sixteen.

Since there was no documentation of her birth from Ethiopia that proved her age either way, the trial was postponed to have Hana's body exhumed for examination. Tests on her teeth and bones, however, were inconclusive and experts couldn't confirm that she was sixteen.

The defense agreed that Larry and Carri may have been bad parents and their choices were bad, but they weren't killers and had no idea that their form of discipline would lead to the child's death.

After seven weeks of testimony, the jury didn't agree with the defense and both Larry and Carri Williams were convicted of first-degree manslaughter and first-degree assault. Carri was also found guilty of homicide by abuse and was sentenced to thirty-seven years in prison. Larry Williams was sentenced to nearly twenty-eight years and given credit for the almost two years he had been in jail awaiting trial.

———

This chapter is a free bonus chapter from True Crime Case Histories: Volume 5

Online Appendix

Visit my website for additional photos and videos pertaining to the cases in this book:

http://TrueCrimeCaseHistories.com/vol8/

Also by Jason Neal

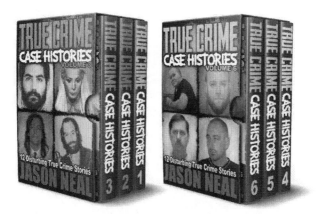

Looking for more?? I am constantly adding new volumes of True Crime Case Histories and all books are also available in paperback, hardcover and audiobooks.

Check out the complete series on Amazon:

Amazon US / Amazon UK

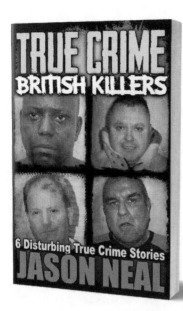

FREE Bonus Book For My Readers

Click to get your free copy!

As my way of saying "Thank you" for downloading, I'm giving away a FREE true crime book I think you'll enjoy.

http://truecrimecasehistories.com

Just click the link above to let me know where to send your free gift!

Choose Your Free True Crime Audiobook

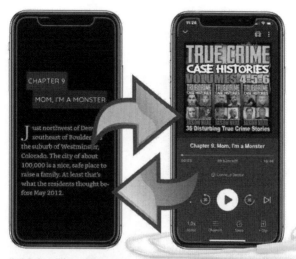

Add Audible Narration and Keep the Story Going!
Plus Get a FREE True Crime Audiobook!

Switch between listening to an audiobook and reading on your Kindle. **Plus choose your first audiobook for FREE!** Audible US / Audible UK

THANK YOU!

Thank you for reading my eighth Volume of True Crime Case Histories. I truly hope you enjoyed it. If you did, I would be sincerely grateful if you would take a few minutes to write a review for me on Amazon using the link below.

http://truecrime.page/book8

I'd also like to encourage you to sign-up for my email list for updates, discounts and freebies on future books! I promise I'll make it worth your while with future freebies.

http://truecrimecasehistories.com

And please take a moment and follow me on Amazon

http://truecrime.page/amazonUS

http://truecrime.page/amazonUK

One last thing. I would love to hear your feedback and personal thoughts on the book. I have found that many people that aren't regular readers of true crime can't handle the horrible details of stories like these. Do you think the level of detail is ok, or would you rather see it toned down a bit? Or if you'd like to contact me for any other reason free to email me at:

jasonnealbooks@gmail.com

https://linktr.ee/JasonNeal

Thanks so much,

Jason Neal

ABOUT THE AUTHOR

Jason Neal is a Best-Selling American True Crime Author living in Hawaii with his Turkish-British wife. Jason started his writing career in the late eighties as a music industry publisher and wrote his first true crime collection in 2019.

As a boy growing up in the eighties just south of Seattle, Jason became interested in true crime stories after hearing the news of the Green River Killer so close to his home. Over the subsequent years he would read everything he could get his hands on about true crime and serial killers.

As he approached 50, Jason began to assemble stories of the crimes that have fascinated him most throughout his life. He's especially obsessed by cases solved by sheer luck, amazing police work, and groundbreaking technology like early DNA cases and more recently reverse genealogy.

amazon.com/author/jason-neal

goodreads.com/jasonneal

bookbub.com/profile/jason-neal

facebook.com/jasonnealauthor

Made in the USA
Columbia, SC
11 May 2022